D0556972

REAL ESTATE INVESTING

George Bockl

Prentice-Hall, Inc.　　　　　Englewood Cliffs, New Jersey

Prentice-Hall International, Inc., *London*
Prentice-Hall of Australia, Pty. Ltd., *Sydney*
Prentice-Hall of Canada, Ltd., *Toronto*
Prentice-Hall of India Private Ltd., *New Delhi*
Prentice-Hall of Japan, Inc., *Tokyo*
Prentice-Hall of Southeast Asia Pte. Ltd., *Singapore*
Whitehall Books, Ltd., *Wellington, New Zealand*

©1977 by

Prentice-Hall, Inc.

Englewood Cliffs, N.J.

*All rights reserved. No part of this book
may be reproduced in any form or by any
means, without permission in writing from
the publisher.*

Originally published as

George Bockl on Real Estate Investing

Reward Edition . . . . . . March 1979

This publication is designed to provide accurate and authoritative information in
regard to the subject matter covered. It is sold with the understanding that the
publisher is not engaged in rendering legal, accounting, or other professional service.
If legal advice or other expert assistance is required, the services of a competent
professional person should be sought.

*. . . From the Declaration of Principles Jointly adopted by a Committee of the
American Bar Association and a Committee of Publishers and Associations.*

Library of Congress Cataloging in Publication Data

Bockl, George
    George Bockl On real estate investing.

    Includes index
    1. Real estate investment. I. Title II. Title:
On real estate investing.
HD1379.B64   332.6'324   77-1490

Printed in the United States of America

To my Editor-in-Chief—
my wife Mildred,
whose deft grammatical touches
smoothed the manuscript's readability.

ABOUT THE AUTHOR

George Bockl, President of George Bockl Enterprises, Milwaukee, Wisconsin, has sold more than $300,000,000 in residential and commercial real estate during the past 30-plus years. He has been involved in real estate investments of all types and sizes including more than 30 conversions of old buildings to new and profitable uses. In addition to the many hundreds of hours he has given to private real estate counseling, Mr. Bockl also teaches real estate and is the author of two best-selling books, HOW TO USE LEVERAGE TO MAKE MONEY IN LOCAL REAL ESTATE and HOW REAL ESTATE FORTUNES ARE MADE, both published by Prentice-Hall, Inc.

READING THIS BOOK
COULD CHANGE
YOUR FINANCIAL FUTURE

This book is about an infrequently used real estate principle which, when fully grasped, could make you independently wealthy.

Let me explain. There are two ways to build a big yearly income in investment real estate. One is to earn money, pay taxes, and invest the residual. The other is what this book is all about.

In the first instance, let's say you've earned $50,000 in some way, beyond your $20,000 salary, and you want to invest it in real estate. First, you'll have to pay about $25,000 in income taxes. The balance could then be invested in property at 10 per cent yield for a $2,500 yearly income.

This is the long and arduous way to create a yearly income. It's awfully difficult to earn $50,000 a year beyond your salary, and even if you do, you can only keep half of it.

Now, let me show you a far shorter and easier way to build a $2,500 yearly income.

An elderly owner is having problems managing a 12-family apartment building. The rent is only $20,000 a year because it's mismanaged. It could easily be $22,500 a year under good management. Let's assume the 12-unit apartment building owner nets $12,500 before debt service. Using what I call the "conduit method" (explained fully in Chapters 1 and 2), you buy the property with some seed money and guarantee the owner a trouble-free, yearly annuity of $11,500 a year, or only $1,000 less than the amount he's presently getting with all the irritating problems of management.

If you have the managerial qualifications, you should be able to bring the rent up from $20,000 to $22,500. This will net $3,500 a year—$1,000 to pay off the seed money, and a $2,500 annuity for your extra layer of alert management.

This is but one example. There are a dozen different ways to *shortcut* into building a big yearly income. For instance, you can net lease a poorly managed apartment building for 15 years and earn a yearly income to the extent of your superior management. One of my salesmen averaged $12,000 a year for 15 years by net leasing a 24-family. There are many profitable variations of this unusual, little used, income-building method.

Or, you can convert an automobile showroom and repair garage into a mini-mall shopping mart and create a yearly $50,000 cash overage. I describe this investment in detail, step by step, in the first chapter. And I can tell you, it's a lot easier than earning $1,000,000, paying half in taxes, and investing the balance to yield $50,000 a year!

There are many ways to create your own projects, and I'll tell you about them in this book. You'll read about a travel guide who financed the building of a quaint resort in Switzerland by bartering future free vacations for carpenters', plumbers', and electricians' moonlighting hours. And you'll read with disbelief how an ordinary electrician bought a theater and stores from a multi-million dollar public company and imaginatively increased its cash flow so that he now enjoys a $50,000 yearly income. And he had to do it with little money—because that's all he had!

You'll say to yourself, "Heck, I can't believe it," when I describe how an auto mechanic bought a community shopping center with next to nothing down, and how he now enjoys a yearly income of $20,000! But you'd better believe it, as the saying goes, because that's exactly what happened. It would have been absolutely impossible for this auto mechanic to earn $400,000, reinvest it after taxes, and get such an income!

Throughout the book you'll be reading not only what others and I have done personally to build a yearly income, but also about the advice I've given to dozens of readers and acquaintances who called, or wrote to me, asking for solutions to knotty real estate problems.

People from 20 different states, Canada, and even the Union of South Africa, posed their problems.

How I unsnarled them, using innovative step-by-step approaches, could help you too, because reading how I solved their problems could give you the answers to your own problems. In each case, I describe the question and offer a specific solution, fitting a particular individual, with the aim of helping him build a stable, dependable, yearly income.

Some of my answers are known to only a few. My reason for sharing them with you in this book is to make them known to many. For the price of this book, you'll have hundreds of thousands of dollars worth of advice, based on my hundreds of hours on the phone with people in many parts of the country.

What's my reward? The sharing of knowledge, as others have shared theirs with me—knowing that you are going to benefit, to better your life.

A word of caution. Any idea, no matter how practical, will boomerang if it's abused. I therefore devote a chapter on what constitutes a prudent project, and another on how to avoid hazardous risks. I offer illustrations to show why some succeed and others fail.

I don't want my readers to go amuck with unreasoned ambition. To discourage that, I show what happens to those who do—in vivid detail. Growing bigger and bigger does not necessarily bring bigger profits. Often it's just the reverse.

I want you to make money—but with prudent restraint—keyed to moral principles. Without that, making money becomes an empty exercise.

I predict—when you digest this book thoroughly—it'll tap your money-making abilities and start your creative juices flowing abundantly.

GEORGE BOCKL

TABLE OF CONTENTS

1

Creating Your Own Projects—The Greatest Money-Making Idea In Real Estate

There are dozens of ways to make money in real estate. Some are easier and more interesting than others. There is brokerage, trading, building and selling, consulting; but the most remunerative is creating and managing your own projects. It is by far the fastest way to create wealth and independence.

Everyone knows that a straight line is the shortest distance between two points, but few know the shortest route to building a big, continuing income in investment real estate. If you want to go from Chicago to Denver, you're not going to drive by way of Dallas. Yet, that's exactly what many people are doing.

The central theme of this book deals with finding the shortest way to create a yearly income in investment real estate.

Let me make an important comparison. Suppose you bought and sold real estate and made $100,000 in one year, or earned $100,000 in some other business, or got a salary of $100,000; your tax would be about $60,000, and you'd have $40,000 left. If you invested it

17

in a high yielding bond with a return of 10 per cent, you'd earn $4,000 a year.

But very few can earn $100,000 a year. It takes prodigious effort and unusual talent to make this huge amount of money as a basis for a $4,000 yearly income.

Now, let me show you a much easier and quicker way to create a $4,000 yearly income. Here are four simple techniques that some of my students are using successfully to build annuities in investment real estate.

CAPITALIZING ON THE POTENTIAL
OF A VACANT BUILDING

Spotting a vacant building, finding a tenant, mortgaging it on the strength of the lease, and developing a cash flow with a little seed money, is a lot easier than earning $100,000.

A student of mine, who was not in the real estate business, optioned a 6,000 square foot empty store for $60,000 after one of my lectures dealing with the availability of opportunities in vacant buildings. He made over a hundred calls until he found a tenant who was willing to pay $24,000 a year rent, providing it was remodeled for offices to his specifications. With a letter of intent in hand, he was able to get a mortgage commitment of $90,000, predicated on his spending $25,000 for remodeling. He closed the deal and wound up with $5,000 in cash and a yearly cash flow of $4,000 after all fixed expenses and debt service.

While this deal required a lot of work in putting all the pieces together, it was still a lot easier than earning $100,000, paying taxes, and investing the residual for a return of $4,000 a year. It takes far less ability to do what that young man did than to be an executive who commands a $100,000 salary. Yet, the monetary results are the same. Why? Because of the revolutionary financial advantage inherent in creating real estate projects. It's by far the quickest and easiest way to build a yearly income.

Obtaining an option was the key to this deal. The consideration for an option (the legal right to buy the property based on the terms of the option) varies from: (1) no money, to (2) little money, or (3) substantial money, depending on the size of the deal and the chances of consummating it. For instance, on a $60,000 deal, the option time could vary from 30 to 90 days, and the amount, from nothing if the deal has little chance of being consummated, to $3,000 if the potential buyer thinks he has a hot deal and an excellent chance of working it out.

NET LEASING AN APARTMENT BUILDING

Another of my students learned how to lease an apartment building from an owner at a net figure, and manage it as if it was his own.

"After listening to Mr. Bockl's lecture on net leasing apartment buildings," he told the class one evening, "I found an elderly couple who, I could see, were mismanaging their twelve-family, either because they didn't have the energy to care for it, or they didn't need the money. They owned it free and clear and were netting about $11,000 a year. I suggested that they lease it to me for $10,000 a year for ten years. I agreed to make necessary repairs to the property, and to keep it well maintained throughout the lease period. In making the presentation, I stressed my handyman's experience and character references—my banker, minister and computer manager who was my superior.

"Their lawyer drew up the papers and we made the deal. I know I'll clear at least $3,000 a year and still have enough to keep the property in good repair. The deal was clinched, I believe, when I said, 'This will be good for you because you'll be free of problems and you'll still receive almost all the money you're now getting. It'll be good for me because by raising some rents, I could earn an extra $3,000 for my family. And it'll be good for the tenants because now they'll get prompt attention to all their needs.' "

This deal was made about ten years ago. With the rise in rents during the last decade, it would not surprise me to find that my student netted at least $6,000 a year during the length of the lease. And I'm going to let you figure out how much money he would have had to earn to enjoy a $6,000 annuity with so little effort and no money of his own.

BUILDING SMALL PROJECTS

On page 191 of my book, *How to Use Leverage to Make Money in Local Real Estate,* I tell how an elderly gentleman used the project method to build a $200,000 yearly income. He put his ideas to work without realizing he had come upon a magic formula. I tell how we became friendly at a commercial real estate seminar, while listening to a panel of experts. It happened about 15 years ago. He whispered in my ear, "Those guys are experts? I could buy and sell any one of 'em. Maybe all of 'em." He had the bluntness of a doer.

Most of them were high-salaried men of big corporations who mastered their specialties and were now sharing their knowledge with real estate men who came from various parts of the country to listen and learn. After the meeting I cornered the old man for his story.

What was his secret? Very simple. He would find an insurance company, or a group of doctors or lawyers who were looking for quarters in a certain location, and he would build to suit. He had the knack of buying a lot at the lowest possible price, finding the small contractor (usually a father-son operation) who had the lowest overhead, arranging financing (after shopping several lenders) with the lowest interest rates, and then packaging the deal for a ten or fifteen year lease. Usually he would mortgage out with a 2 per cent cash flow, that is $2,000 yearly overage after fixed expenses and debt service on a typical $100,000 building. He probably didn't realize it, but every time he concluded a simple deal like that, it was equivalent to earning about $50,000.

Well, this man continued making these little deals until he had provided for the financial futures of his salaried, college-educated children, and all of his grandchildren. He still had a $200,000 yearly income for himself.

There was no other way he could possibly have earned the millions that would have been required to build his investment portfolio. He had no special qualifications. He was not articulate, and would have been hard put to find a $15,000-a-year job. But he chanced upon a magic formula—a quick, money-making method—creating his own projects.

BUYING ON A LAND CONTRACT
WITH LITTLE MONEY DOWN

Buying property on a land contract, with little money down, is another easy way to build a yearly income in investment real estate. There are plenty of such opportunities. If you keep your eyes and ears open, you'll see and hear more of them, especially after you read how easily it's done and how much it's worth when you've done it.

There are hundreds of landlords in each city with "short fuses." They find it difficult to get along with tenants, and "blow up" when the complaints become unreasonable. Usually they don't make good managers, and their properties show it—vacancies, neglect, losses. If you're wide awake, their problems can become your opportunities. But where are those "troubled" properties and "troubled" landlords? How do you find them?

Perk up when you read about a landlord being cited by a court for neglecting his property, or about a landlord-tenant fracas. Such incidents provide reasons for selling. Or if you hear a bit of gossip such as, "I like my place but I hate my landlord," check it out. If you're in the company of a landlord, especially an elderly one who complains, "I've had it up to here," in relating his real estate woes, go after him. Relieve him of his troubles by suggesting the conditional sales approach, with a small down payment; that is, you're willing to buy his property on a land contract—without a warranty deed. That means that if you don't make payments promptly, he can get you out of the property promptly, unlike a warranty deed which would give you more rights and more time to stall a foreclosure.

Tell the owner about yourself, your hopes and dreams, and how you're willing to work hard to realize them. Build up your character, it's your most valuable asset when you're short of money. (Of course, if you're short on character, the owner isn't going to entrust a big chunk of his fortune to you.) It's important that he feels comfortable with you. You can clinch your presentation with, "I'll really be working for you, because I intend to pay each month about what you're netting now. What I earn will have to come out of the extra work and care I give your property."

This line of presentation applies to duplexes, four-families, perhaps up to 20 units, where the owners and buyers are relatively unsophisticated. In larger properties, the same integrity principle can be applied too, but more finesse and explanation is needed.

About ten years ago, I decided to get rid of some "cats and dogs," which I had accumulated during my real estate trading days. My property manager was doing less than a good job in managing them, and a young man who had somehow got wind of it, came to my office and said much the same things I just told you.

"I'm young, handy, and reliable. I could do a good job on your marginal real estate. Your manager has shown them to me, and the way he talks, they're your headache properties. I don't have much money, but I'd sure like to work out a deal with you."

He did. I sold him 30 scattered units on a land contract for $97,000, with $5,000 down. The rents were $45,000 a year. After $25,000 in repairs, taxes, etc. we netted $20,000. We owned them free and clear. His payments were $1,700 a month, including interest and principal, interest at 6 per cent. We were getting slightly more than we were netting.

But the young man, being his own repairman, was earning about $15,000 a year, plus amortizing about $15,000 a year on principal. It was more than he had ever earned in his life. It was a good deal for him, for us, and for the tenants. He took better care of them than we did, because his entire livelihood was at stake, and he therefore gave them his entire personal attention.

Please do not conclude from the foregoing that salaried people, who earn ordinary incomes, and can't take advantage of self-created tax shelters, do not play an important role in our society. We could not get along without them. I'm only suggesting different ways to add to that ordinary income. And please don't get the idea that the short cuts I've described are in any way an encouragement to evade taxes. Avoiding them for the time being, yes, that's legal, but evading them, no, that's illegal. Keep in mind that Uncle Sam will get you in the end, anyway, when you sell your property or when your estate is probated. And that's as it should be. You should be willing to pay your share for the freedoms you enjoy and the protection you receive from your government.

THE ANATOMY OF A SELF-CREATED PROJECT
THAT WILL YIELD $40,000 A YEAR
WITH ONLY $10,000 SEED MONEY

Not enough people know how to cash in on the permanence of steel, brick, and mortar. With a little money and lots of imagination, a building, like few other things, can keep yielding income for generations.

Fifty years ago, a wholesale grocer expanded his business into a new steel and concrete, six-story, 100,000 square foot building. Thirty years later, the business folded, and the executor of the estate sold it for a reported $100,000 to a candy salesman. The new owner flirted with some uses for it, but without success. When I suggested a 99-year lease, he listened. We were both amateurs at the time, and since he was anxious to bail out of the vacant building, and I to get into a challenging deal, we settled for an annual rental of $28,000 for the first 10 years, $20,000 for the next 10 years, and $15,000 for the remaining 79 years.

This turned out to be an excellent deal for him. With my lease in hand, he borrowed the $100,000 he paid for the building, and amortized it in 20 years at the then prevailing rate of 5 per cent interest, creating a cash flow of about $20,000 a year. That's not bad for an amateur. That deal gave him his start towards a successful real estate career. That's what the building did for him.

Here is what it did for me. After a few months of intensive searching, I fell into a bit of luck. The U.S. Army was looking for a training center of about 60,000 square feet. They liked my building, and signed a five-year lease for $40,000 a year. Using the army's lease as collateral, I borrowed $65,000 from a bank to build partitions, hang light fixtures, and install a passenger elevator—improvements the brass insisted on before signing the lease. I soon rented the balance of some 40,000 square feet to a plastic manufacturing company for $25,000 a year. In three years I payed off the bank loan from the overage, and cleared $20,000 yearly for two subsequent years. At the termination of its lease, the army moved out and the plastic company went bankrupt. I had a vacant building again.

But the steel, brick, and mortar was still potentially productive. The problem was to find a new user. After nine months of thrashing for tenants and absorbing losses, I leased the entire building to a wholesale merchandizing firm for 10 years. It payed all expenses, including the $28,000-a-year leasehold rent and $10,000-a-year net to me. Not good, but not bad either.

Seven years later, the merchandizing firm sold out to a national chain and payed me $75,000 to release it from the remaining three years of the lease. I had a vacant building again and $75,000 in cash.

My search for tenants began all over again. This time a social agency leased 75 per cent of the building for 10 years, and soon afterward, two other tenants filled it. This produced a cash flow of about $20,000 a year again, but I had to spend about $150,000 in improvements to get the leases.

I decided I had had enough of the building and sold my leasehold interest to an associate for $150,000 with nothing down, but on the following terms: He was to obtain a $75,000 first mortgage and turn over the proceeds to me so that with my $75,000 on hand, I could pay for the $150,000 in improvements. He signed a second mortgage for $75,000 in my favor. His payments on the first and second mortgages were about $15,000 a year, leaving him a $5,000 yearly income. Not bad, considering that he got a fully occupied building, with no money of his own in it.

Ten years later, the story takes an interesting turn. In 1974, the social agency moved out and my friend was faced with a $4,000-a-month deficit, a balance of $35,000 on the first mortgage, and a $50,000 balance on my second mortgage. For six months he tried to lease the building to one big user, then to lease by floors, then by parts of floors. All he got were no's and maybe's.

One day he called, "George, I'm giving you back your building. It's not my cup of tea."

I knew what that meant. He would simply hand me the stock which I had conveyed to him with no down payment—and walk out of the deal. That was his legal right. I had a choice of either assuming the $4,000 monthly deficit and the $35,000 first mortgage balance, or of taking a walk with him and turning the building back to the candy salesman. I had no legal obligation to continue making up the deficits or to assume the first mortgage balance. The $50,000 second mortgage which my associate owed me was, of course, automatically wiped out.

While I was squirming in indecision as to whether to take the building or drop it, I called the former candy salesman, the prime lessor, to see if he would be willing to assume the $50,000 second mortgage and the $35,000 first mortgage, if I nullified the balance of the 99-year lease. He would then become the owner of the building once more—without a lessee.

"No," he said, "I'd rather leave things as they are."

I couldn't tell whether he was planning to get the building back without assuming the $50,000 due me, or whether he just didn't want the risks of becoming the owner of an almost vacant building.

This was happening at a time when I was preparing to write this book for Prentice-Hall. What better way of proving that creating a project is a short cut to building a big yearly income than actually doing it myself during a difficult real estate year while writing this book? I figured it would add a convincing note to my writing.

I took the building back and went to work to prove my theory. It was 1974—a depression year in real estate. Our economy was in the doldrums. The doldrums! That gave me an idea.

I prepared an article for our metropolitan newspaper, suggesting that while office tenants were always moving up in the affluent sixties, they were going to move down in the austere seventies. To prove it, I said in the article, I'm going to convert a loft building into office space to rent at $2.00 a square foot—half the prevailing rate of B buildings and a third of Class A buildings. Those with pinching budgets, I hinted, would step down to save expenses.

The article appeared on the front page of the real estate section. I sent 1,000 cards and made about 100 calls stressing the austerity theme of the article. I placed a daily ad under "Office Space for Rent," which read:

PRIVATE OFFICES
$20 A MONTH
OPEN SPACE—$2.00 SQ.FT.
Call GEORGE BOCKL 272-0069

The combined promotional campaign brought a flurry of responses. Commercial artists, photographers, small advertising agencies, and tenants who were working out of their homes to cut expenses, flocked to look at my building. As of this writing (mid-1976) the rent roll is $90,000 a year and the building is 65 per cent occupied. By the time this book is published, I'm sure the gross rent will be $150,000 a year, which will give me a cash flow of about $50,000 a year.

This will have been accomplished with an expenditure of only $90,000 in added improvements. Creating a yearly income of $50,000 is equivalent to earning about $1,000,000, paying taxes and investing the balance at 10 per cent. I can assure you, it's a lot easier finding tenants at $2.00 a square foot than making $1,000,000.

My very capable associate and friend, who walked out of the deal, earns upward of $85,000 a year in brokerage, and is a nationally recognized lecturer in investment real estate. But he didn't fully realize that filling that building was equivalent to making $1,000,000. Why didn't he do it? I don't know. Either he didn't see the economics I have just described, or he didn't want to face the deficits. Or perhaps he enjoyed brokerage more than fussing with management and listening to tenants' complaints.

A DEAL I COULDN'T REFUSE

Across the street from my office was a neglected automobile body shop which cast a blighting shadow on the well-kept adjoining buildings. Less than a block away, an automobile showroom and a used car lot didn't do the neighborhood any good either. These three separate parcels were owned by a retired businessman who was now renting them for $65,000 a year to a Chevrolet dealer. The Chevrolet lease was expiring in mid-1975, and the owner put his property on the market in 1973 for $800,000. It was ridiculously high. In 1974, he still was hoping that someone would see unusual values in the sites if not in the buildings. But 1974 was not a good building year, and he was getting no offers.

In the spring of 1975, the broker handling those properties came to my office and said, "You've done a great job converting this warehouse (in which my office was located) into a modern office building. Why don't you see what you can do with the three Chevrolet parcels. You'd be upgrading your neighborhood and adding value to your office building as well. You're innovative—find a use."

"Like what?" I asked.

"Well, I don't know, but I'm sure you'll come up with something."

He wasn't very convincing, but his next remark was more arousing.

"What if you could get the properties for $400,000? I think I could resell the used car lot to a hamburger franchise for $150,000 and the body garage to a pizza franchise for $100,000. That would leave the 40,000 square foot showroom for only $150,000."

"Let me think about it," I said.

I wanted to upgrade the area, but I was skeptical whether the fast-food restaurants would do it. When I checked with the watchdog neighborhood association about the two fast-food restaurants, the officers said, "We'd object."

The broker was pressing me for an answer, and in one of my rash moments I offered $350,000. It was accepted.

Let me qualify my rashness. It was an unusually low price, and now that the chips were down, I had a hunch that somehow I'd come up with the right answer. However, I don't recommend this intuitive rashness for neophytes.

With the closing date set for September, I began thinking in earnest. Next door to the dilapidated body shop was a successful Ford agency whose buildings were kept up immaculately. They were a credit to the neighborhood. I knew that there had been some negotiations between the seller and the Ford dealer, and I wanted to find out why nothing came of them.

"Why didn't you buy it," I asked the president.

"Very simple. The price was too high."

"Look," I said, putting my cards on the table, "I paid only $350,000 for the three properties, and I can sell the body shop to you for an awfully low price."

"Like what?"

"Like $125,000."

"You'll have my answer in a few days."

They bought it. It was probably $75,000 below the previous asking price.

Now I was left with the 40,000 square foot showroom garage and a 30,000 square foot used car lot across the street for $225,000. What could I do now? I borrowed $200,000 when I closed the deal and waited for an idea. None came.

In the meantime, the broker who sold me the properties called and said that the hamburger company might be willing to pay $175,000 for the used car lot. Would I take it? It was very tempting. I could own the showroom, the best of the three parcels, for a mere $50,000! But what about the neighbors and my own responsibility to the neighborhood? Nevertheless, it was an offer not easy to refuse.

Just about this time, while doing some research for this book, I came across a magazine which described the conversion of vacant buildings into mini-malls. It was something new—a creative response to the need for new uses for vacant buildings.

I had a vacant building. Why not use it as another example of starting from scratch and building a yearly income? Here was a challenging idea that would read convincingly well in my book. Even though I was over my ears with converting the wholesale grocery into

an office building, I couldn't resist doing the "mall"—for my readers
for the community and for the yearly income.

Here was my economic rationale for doing it. Note it carefully,
because you'll have many opportunities to analyze similar situations.
It's one of the new investment forms that's going to sweep the country.

I concluded, after making a careful examination of the 40,000
square feet of space, that I would have 30,000 square feet of net
rentable selling space, after allowing for three generous, meandering
malls, washrooms, and stairwells. Three malls, because there were
10,000 square feet that sloped into a lower level, 23,000 square feet on
the main floor, and 7,000 square feet of mezzanine.

I assumed I could lease the space at $5 a square foot for a total of
$150,000 a year. I projected my remodeling cost at $275,000, and with
a cost of $225,000 for the garage and parking lot, my total for the
project would be about $500,000. I figured $16,000 for taxes, and
$12,000 a year for heat, light, air conditioning, water, snow removal,
security, etc., with the tenants paying for all escalations based on the
number of square feet of their stores, above my two base figures of
$16,000 and $12,000. I added another $12,000 a year for
management. This totaled about $40,000 a year for fixed expenses.

I projected a mortgage of $500,000 at 9 per cent and a 25 year
amortization for a debt service of about $55,000 a year. If all my
projections were correct, I would have no trouble getting such a loan
since I would be left with a cash flow of $55,000 a year after fixed
expenses and debt service. And what I particularly liked about my
projections was that I wouldn't have a penny of my own money in the
deal.

You can now see why I couldn't resist going into it, especially
when I found in my research that 45,000 people lived within a one
mile radius of my property, that 50 per cent of them earned $15,000 a
year and up, and 15,000 cars passed it daily. I was grateful I had
heeded the neighbor association's wishes and hadn't sold the lot to a
hamburger franchise because without its 100 parking stalls, my
project could never have gotten off the ground.

Having decided to go ahead, I alerted my bank that I might need
another $300,000 for interim financing. I offered to sign it personally
because converting a garage into stores was plowing new real estate
ground, and I didn't expect them to exculpate me in the event the

project went sour. I put a half million of the bank's money on the line and went to work.

How do you let people know what you're trying to do? That's important—most important! Well, using the public media—television, radio and newspapers—is the quickest way to get attention, and it's wonderful because it costs nothing. I used all three. How? I called the real estate editor of the *Milwaukee Journal* and told him my story.

"Hey, that's news," he said. "A garage building into an enclosed shopping mall? But, George, give me your word that you're not fishing for a story to use as a trial balloon. Are you definitely going ahead with it?"

"You have my word."

He ran the story on the front page of the Sunday Real Estate Section with a colored rendering showing how the mall was going to look when finished. A week later, the leading television station called me, and within hours its crew rolled their film while I pointed to the garage building and described, in glowing terms, how I was going to convert it into some thirty unusual shops.

"What kind of shops?" the interviewer asked.

What a great leading question, I thought. Here was my chance to tell the hundreds of thousands of viewers what stores I wanted.

"Quaint restaurants, antique shops, men's apparel, arts, crafts, unusual glassware, lamps, macramé, a florist, maybe a mini theater..."

Several days later I called the leading radio station.

"I'd be willing to appear on your talk show if you think the mall idea would be of interest to your listeners."

I took it for granted that with the newspaper and television exposure, the radio manager knew what I was talking about. He did. I got half an hour of free time to explain what kind of stores I wanted in the mall. Lest you get the idea that I "used" the media, let me say that I gave as much as I received. The media are hungry for news, for the unusual—they need grist for their news mills. I gave them the grist, they gave me visibility.

But I didn't stop there. I printed a beautiful, three-color brochure and sent it to some 500 store owners. I placed an ad in both daily papers which read:

STORES FOR RENT
IN PROSPECT MALL
ON PROSPECT NEAR NORTH AVE.
We have an excellent location for a restaurant,
men's wear, antiques, glassware, arts, crafts,
candies, small grocery, smoke shop, or anything
you have to sell. 15,000 cars pass it daily. 45,000
people live within 1 mile radius. 50% earn over
$15,000 a year. For details call
GEORGE BOCKL ENTERPRISES   272-0069

Within 30 days, I received about 100 calls as a result of my
various promotions. Most were skeptical about renting stores in an
old garage, but enough were willing to chance it in the hope of
pioneering something new. While in construction, I signed leases for a
greeting card, gift-and-book shop, an old-fashioned ice cream parlor,
a family restaurant, a florist, a picture framer, a small grocery
store and two mini movie theaters. I had enough calls so that I could
choose stores which met the needs of the community. And if there was
a product or service which I felt the neighbors needed, but the would-
be proprietor was short of capital, I offered to help arrange a loan so
he could get into my mall.

As this book goes to press, I can safely say that my chances of
success are excellent, in spite of austere economic conditions. Perhaps
I should say because of the austere conditions, because by buying an
old building cheaply and recycling it, I was able to lease space at half
the price the major shopping centers were charging. Also working in
my favor was the trend toward more personalized, small, community
stores, which people prefer to huge, regional, impersonal, shopping
centers 10 to 15 miles away. At any rate, I hope I've made the point
that it's a lot easier to convert a garage building into an enclosed mall
to net a $55,000 yearly income than to earn a million dollars, pay taxes
and invest it at 10 per cent. My loft building project, and now the
mall, should certainly convince you that developing projects is a
revolutionary short cut to building big, continuing yearly incomes.
I've gone into these two projects to get fresh material for my book and
to share my findings with you. If they're successful, as I'm sure they
will be, they'll prove that sharing knowledge is not only rewarding, but
profitable as well.

AN INNOVATIVE YOUNG MAN BUILDS A YEARLY INCOME
OUT OF A MULTI-MILLION-DOLLAR COMPANY'S MISTAKE

In 1968, a savings-and-loan association authorized a $600,000 mortgage to build the Phoenix, a 40,000 square foot office building. It was a big mistake. Three reasons made it a bad loan—mediocre location, a crunch in the economy, and an over-extended developer. The developer ran out of money when the building was 80 per cent completed, and the lender foreclosed. For six years, the savings-and-loan company tried to sell the vacant folly. Its costs climbed to $900,000. There seemed to be no answer—no one wanted it.

I called Wallace, a young man who read my books and put some of their ideas to work.

"You've been creative in small projects. I'd like to suggest a big one—the Phoenix Building."

"But that's been a white elephant for years."

"That's why I'm calling you. Some of the best deals have come out of white elephants. Try to do something with it."

"Like what?"

"Like taking an option for six months and trying to lease it, and then buying it if you're successful."

That's all I said. He did the rest.

The savings-and-loan association was losing about $60,000 a year holding on to their "mistake." Wallace offered $5,000 for a six-month option to lease the Phoenix, with the provision that if he filled it 50 per cent, he would have the right to buy it for $750,000 with $100,000 down. The option also provided that the lender was to advance finishing costs for all improvements needed to get the tenants into the building. The multi-million-dollar company agreed—what alternative did it have? It was getting tired of losing $60,000 a year, of seeing its sinking loan sink deeper into an empty building.

Wallace went to work. He made 1,000 cold-turkey calls. When his option expired, he had leased only 30 per cent of the space. But they didn't cut him off. The officers of the savings-and-loan saw how hard he worked on their "dog" property, and wisely extended the option for another six months. In appreciation of their confidence in him, Wallace redoubled his efforts, and by the end of the year, he leased 65 per cent of the building.

It was a magnificent job, but Wallace could not afford to buy the building for $750,000 because at $5.50 a square foot and a $650,000 mortgage at 9 per cent for 25 years, it still showed about a $20,000 loss. The break-even point was about 80 per cent occupancy. Wallace realized that in his enthusiasm, he hadn't thought the deal through thoroughly.

He made them this proposition. He'd buy it with $100,000 down and assume a $650,000 mortgage, provided they would charge him only 2 per cent interest until he was 85 per cent occupied, and continue to pay for the improvements as he got new tenants. He showed them why the original proposition would not be fair—he would be showing a loss after all his hard work. By this time, they no longer looked at the deal on a strictly commercial basis. They found themselves cheering the young man on. Didn't he pull the Phoenix out of the ashes and give it life? They accepted his new proposition.

"But," he said when the details were worked out, "you'll have to give me 60 days to raise the $100,000. I don't have it." They agreed to that too.

Here's how Wallace ingeniously got the $100,000. He offered the following deal to two doctors who were in a high income tax bracket. He agreed to sell each of them one third of his equity for $50,000 and give him 45 per cent of the depreciation. With the low interest rate of 2 per cent, the building was already breaking even at 65 per cent occupancy, and since the doctors controlled 90 per cent of the depreciation, they could show substantial losses against their ordinary income. That would be their return until Wallace filled the building. At that time there would be about a $30,000 cash flow, after fixed expenses, and debt service on $650,000 at 9 per cent based on 25 years amortization. This would make it an excellent deal for the doctors, and they agreed. Wallace got the $100,000 and bought the Phoenix Building.

As of this writing, the building is 80 per cent filled, and when I checked with Wallace, he said he had enough prospects to fill it within 90 days. I'm sure he will. You can't stop a young man with that kind of stick-to-itiveness. When that happens, each doctor will have a tax-sheltered return of $10,000 for his $50,000 investment, Wallace will have a $10,000 yearly income plus $10,000 a year for managing the Phoenix, and the savings-and-loan company will have $100,000 in cash and a 9 per cent return on $650,000 instead of losing $60,000 a year in a deteriorating building.

Wallace worked very hard building his yearly income, but he gained more than income. He proved he could do a difficult job. Investors are now looking at him with new, well-earned respect. Many propositions are being offered to him, and he enjoys the luxury of waiting to pick the right one. Only in his thirties, he's grasped the magical monetary difference betweeen creating his own projects and earning ordinary income. Understanding the revolutionary significance of this annuity-building real estate principle should enable him to advance quickly into independent wealth.

HOW ONE OF MY STUDENTS OUTDID HIS TEACHER

Harry, a young contractor, attended my real estate lectures regularly and read my books thoroughly.

"I want to fuse my contracting with real estate," he said after class one evening. "Creating my own projects fascinates me. Think I can do it?"

"Why not—especially with your contracting experience."

I gave him one assist and away he went. There was a vacant 18,000 square foot Cadillac-agency garage building that a retired owner had been trying to sell for three years. With Harry in mind, I called the owner one day.

"Should I tell you why you haven't sold your Cadillac garage yet?"

"Yeh. I'd like to know."

"Your $200,000 cash price is unrealistic."

"What is realistic?"

"$125,000."

"Got someone?"

"I'll send a contractor over. Perhaps you and he could work something out."

They met and liked each other. And their needs were complementary. The elderly owner wanted to decompress; the contractor wanted to accelerate. The former Cadillac dealer gave Harry a 90 day option at a price of $125,000. Harry must have convinced the elderly owner that he was a go-getter, that he would work hard to make the deal.

Harry didn't lose any time before applying what I stressed in my books and lectures—he made 50 cold-turkey calls a day. Within a month he got a lead that a state government agency was looking for

10,000 square feet of moderately priced office space for handling truant and problem teenagers. Being a contractor, he was quickly able to draw a plan showing them how he could build their needs into his building at $4 a square foot, including heat, light and air conditioning. They accepted and gave him a letter of intent for a 10-year lease.

Armed with $400,000 of secured rental, he went to a savings-and-loan association and arranged for a $225,000 mortgage with a provision that it would advance $125,000 upon signing of the formal lease and closing of the deal; $50,000 when the remodeling was completed and the agency moved in; and the remaining $50,000 when the rest of the 8,000 square feet were rented and remodeled. By the time the deal closed, Harry had beaten enough bushes to flush out another tenant—a successful antique dealer—and leased the remaining 8,000 square feet for $20,000 a year.

When the deal was closed and both tenants moved in, Harry showed me his operating statement. After debt service and fixed expenses, it showed a yearly $10,000 cash flow on a zero investment. He did everything right and benefited all the parties involved. The elderly car dealer got his cash, the government and the antique dealer enjoyed modern space at a low price, the lender made a safe loan, the blight of a vacant building was arrested, and Harry built himself a trouble-free yearly income of $10,000 without a dime of his own money.

But that's only the beginning. My lectures on trading also fascinated him.

"You know," Harry told me after he masterminded a most unusual exchange, "trading does accelerate equities in geometric proportion as you once told us, and I've used it to the hilt."

Here's how he outdid his teacher. Before the ink was dry on the antique dealer's lease, he made a master move. He knew Jerry, a young man who owned three "trouble" properties: a tavern with a huge vacant hall, a vacant 8,000 square foot garage and a 50x150 lot—all in different locations. In his hobnobbing with Jerry, he heard him complain how difficult it was to get tenants for third-rate properties, and how his in particular were losing money for him.

"Jerry," Harry said one day, "I've got a great idea."

"Will it benefit you or me?" he asked breezily.

"Both of us."

"O.K. I'm all ears."

"How would you like to trade your losing properties for my remodeled Cadillac Building?"

"I'd be interested, but you'd better explain it to my father first. He won't let me make a move without him."

Obviously, Jerry was no Harry. He didn't have the stamina or the courage to be turned down several hundred times before finding tenants for his vacant properties. Harry made use of this when he said to Jerry's father:

"I know Jerry would rather have a stable income than fool around with his vacant properties. I've got a plan that'll help us both."

"What's your plan?" the elderly man asked.

"I'll turn over my Cadillac building subject to my $225,000 mortgage to Jerry, and he turns over his tavern building, garage, and lot, free and clear, to me. He's losing $5,000 a year on his properties; by trading, he makes $10,000 a year cash flow plus amortization."

The old man saw the logic of the deal and didn't offer much resistance. This made both Harry and Jerry happy. Especially Harry. He remembered the needs of several prospects he had called in trying to lease the Cadillac garage, and they matched the empty hall and vacant garage building. His hunch worked.

As soon as the trade was consummated, he followed up his leads and leased the empty hall to a dance group and the garage to a chemical laboratory. He needed about $50,000 to remodel both buildings, so he sold the vacant lot to an adjoining office building owner for parking. The happy result of this wheeling and dealing, remodeling and trading, was that Harry was left with two free-and-clear properties which netted him $20,000 a year. A remarkable feat for a small contractor, who accomplished in 18 months what would have taken many years of successful contracting (after taxes) to match.

Junior and senior executives—if you want to know what made Harry run—read Chapter 7 on trading in my book, *How Real Estate Fortunes Are Made.* When you combine that knowledge with creating your own projects, the results can be unbelievably rewarding. I'd like to emphasize that you can hold on to your $20,000- or $30,000-a-year jobs and still do what Harry did. The chances are that what you're doing takes more savvy than what he did.

Don't give up your jobs, but give Harry's experience some thought. Remember, he built his $20,000-a-year income while conducting a full-scale contracting business.

2

The Conduit Technique— A Variation of the Greatest Money-Making Idea in Real Estate

When interest rates soar and money becomes scarce, don't fold your arms and wait for times to change. Get rid of stagnation by creating new patterns of thinking.

The concept of leverage is not dead. True, it can't be used the same way as it was when I wrote my first book, *How to Use Leverage to Make Money In Local Real Estate,* ten years ago, but with a variation which I call the "conduit method," it can be used advantageously today.

It can overcome the money scarcity by unfreezing billions of dollars of new capital. It can break up the log jam of real estate doldrums. It can fling up hundreds of thousands of new buyers and sellers. How?

The concept is simple. We must educate sellers to become mortgagees. That is, show them how to make a sale without resorting to third-party financing. There are billions to be tapped if sellers' equities are used to finance buyers, instead of having to pay the exorbitant deal-killing interest rates of banks, insurance companies and building-and-loan associations.

But, you say, it's an old idea. True! But wait. The old idea becomes a new idea if the sale between buyer and seller is salted with a higher than normal price and peppered with a lower than normal interest rate. This spicing produces a real estate concoction that's good for the seller and excellent for the buyer. And the public benefits too, because stagnant equities are released to flow into new hands. Movement replaces inertia. But enough of generalities. Let me illustrate with an actual example.

HOW AN AUTO MECHANIC WILL BECOME A MILLIONAIRE AT 58

An elderly owner wants to sell a 70,000 square foot community shopping center that nets $90,000 a year before debt service. He is trying to sell it for $1,200,000 in cash and can't. I tell him his chances of getting it are as good as threading a camel through the eye of a needle. I then offer a sales plan that runs something like this: "Sell your shopping center for $1,200,000 with $50,000 down and payments of $70,000 a year to include interest and principal, interest at 4 per cent." After I explain the advantages of selling his property in this manner to a stable young conduit, the elderly owner says, "All right. Find me that young man."

I did. He came into my office with his wife, and made one of the most effective sales presentations I have ever heard....

"My name is Tom Boyd. I'm 35 years old. I run an auto-body shop which nets me $20,000 a year, but by the time I get through with taxes, I don't have much left. I'm young, ambitious, and hard-working. I have the ability to do more than merely manage an auto shop. I know how to handle people and I'm extremely methodical. My wife is my bookkeeper, and together with our two small children, we make a great team. If you're looking for a reliable, stable conduit, I'm your man."

The next day I went to the owner of the shopping center to describe my "find."

"I'm sure you're convinced by now that it's impossible to sell your shopping center for cash. If a buyer has to resort to third party financing with 10 per cent interest, you'd have to cut the price to $600,000, and that's ridiculous, because it would cost twice that much to reproduce it."

"And that's what I want for it, two times $600,000, or $1,200,000."

"I think I can get it for you, if you'll take $70,000 a year payment, 4 per cent interest and $50,000 down. And before you begin squirming again about the low down payment and low interest rate, let me describe the young man who's going to be your insurance policy for a continuing stream of income." After I ticked off his attributes, I said, "Your choice is between getting $600,000 in cash, or selling it to the young man for $1,200,000 based on the terms outlined. With the conduit I got for you, you'd be foolish to cut your price in half.

"O.K.," he said with a big grin, "let's meet the conduit."

I knew the seller would be as impressed with Tom as I was. My job now was to sell the buyer on paying $1,200,000.

"Tom," I began, "let me explain the shopping center deal slowly, and you listen carefully. To reproduce it today would cost over a million dollars—that's point number one. Yet, because of today's high interest rates, you couldn't afford to pay more than $600,000 in cash—that's point number two. But if you could buy it for $1,200,000, with $50,000 down and 4 per cent interest on the balance, you'd be getting a bargain—that's point number three. Let me explain why it's a bargain. First, you'd be paying less interest at 4 per cent on the $1,200,000 ($48,000 a year), than at 10 per cent on $600,000 ($60,000). Second, based on the present operating statement, you'd be left with a cash flow of $20,000 to $30,000 a year. That's a fantastic return on a $50,000 cash investment. Third, in less than 20 years, when you'll be 58, you'll own it free and clear. It's a deal you can't afford to pass. But I've got to sell you to the seller—that's the key point in the deal—more important than price or rate of interest. Fortunately, you have the qualifications. If all this makes sense to you, then let me see what I can do."

"It does, and I'm ready to meet the seller any time you say."

They met, and in a few months, the deal was consummated substantially on the terms I've described. Both parted on a note of exuberance. The seller traded in his managerial burdens for a steady income, and Tom gladly accepted them for tne chance to insure his future.

It's two years since the deal was made, and both seller and buyer
keep thanking me for meeting their needs. The innovative combination of doubling the price, cutting the interest rate, finding an
elderly seller and a young buyer, and subsituting equity financing for
third-party mortgaging, made this interesting transaction possible.
It's leveraging with a vengeance. Yet, it's a safe deal for all parties
involved. It's one way of breaking out of smothering stagnation and
combating the inflationary price of money.

HOW TO BUY A SHOPPING CENTER
WITHOUT THIRD-PARTY FINANCING

Flushed with the success of proving my real estate theory in
actual practice, I went looking for bigger game. I didn't have far to
look. There are dozens of stagnant deals impaled on exorbitant interest rates. Sellers and buyers are stymied by impossible third-party
financing.

John, a wealthy 68-year-old owner of a shopping center, wanted
to be rid of the harassing management details of 250,000 square feet
of real estate, comprising some 50 stores. To compound his problem,
he had to answer to two silent partners, each of whom owned one-
third interest. It was a perfect setup to test my conduit theory.

The first step was to find the right conduit. He couldn't be too
young because the deal needed seasoned executive management and
at least $300,000 in cash. Few have these prerequisites in their early
thirties. After weeks of sifting, I decided on a young man in his early
forties. He was a mortgage banker drawing a fat salary who would
know how to deal with hard-hitting proprietors and chain executives.
What led me to him was a remark he made to me one day.

"George, I'm trapped. I earn too much money to quit my job, yet
I yearn to put my teeth into something I can call my own."

I invited him to lunch and after a few preliminaries, reminded
him of his remark.

"Lowell," I said, "I need a man with ability, guts and $300,000.
If you've got all three, I can structure a deal that's tailor-made for
you—if you're serious about getting out of your comfortable trap."

"What's the deal?"

"There's a shopping center that needs to be sold. (I named it. He
knew it.) The gross rent is $750,000 a year. The net before debt service

is $500,000. I may be able to sell it to you on a land contract for $6,600,000 with payments of $400,000 a year, to include interest and principal, interest at 5 per cent. That will leave you $100,000 a year cash flow for a $300,000 investment. How does it sound so far?"

"I like everything except the $6,600,000 price. It's not worth it."

"I agree. But it's a bargain if the financing can be arranged at 5 per cent interest. And especially when you can get $100,000 cash flow on a $300,000 investment.

"Can you document the $750,000 gross rent and the $250,000 expenses?"

"Those are the figures I was given by the owner. Let's say the deal will be predicated on their certification."

"I'm not saying yes, and I'm not saying no. It's an interesting concept, but highly unorthodox. I haven't run across sales where the price is almost double and the interest rate cut in half. I have to give it some thought—what the consequences are down the pike—5, 10, 15 years from now."

"I want you to give it a lot of thought, just as I did before I picked you from a dozen prospects. You see, I can't sell this shopping center, with only $300,000 down, unless I present the owner with a capable conduit to insure the payout of the remaining $6,300,000. I think you'd make a good one."

"So now I'm a conduit. What's that?" he asked breezily.

The question gave me a chance to explain my theory, and hammer home the point that if I could sell him to the owner, he'd be set financially for life—in a style only super executives of corporations ever attain. When I finished, I knew I had a receptive buyer.

"Go ahead," he said, "try and sell me to the owner."

"John," I began when I sat down with the elderly owner, "I have a great plan for selling your shopping center. You've been trying to sell it for $5,000,000 for over a year, but couldn't. Know why? The 10 per cent interest is the stopper. Your $500,000 net before debt service will just about make the yearly payments on a $4,000,000 mortgage at ten per cent with a 20-year amortization. Why should anyone invest a million dollars for zero cash flow?"

"Then what do you suggest?" he asked. "What's your big idea?"

"Sell it for $6,600,000."

"Be serious. What's the catch?"

"No catch. I can sell your center for $6,600,000 if you're ready to take $300,000 down and the balance of $6,300,000 at 5 per cent with payments of $400,000 a year to include interest and principal

"Wait a minute. Let me get it straight. Aren't you in effect trading a lower interest rate for a higher price?"

"That's right."

"But why so little down? And how good is the man buying it?"

That's exactly what I'd hoped he'd ask. By the time I finished describing Lowell, the elderly owner was convinced the center would be in stronger hands than his.

"What about personal liability?" John asked. The question indicated I was making headway.

"I don't think the buyer would or should assume the balance of $6,300,000 personally. I'd suggest his liability be limited to $200,000 at point of default."

"Let's hold that in abeyance for now. But what happens in case he dies?"

"A $200,000 life insurance policy naming you as the beneficiary should solve that."

"Another question. Foreclosure procedure sometimes takes a year or more. With only $300,000 down, he could pull out most of it before I got the center back."

"You're going to sell it on a land contract, or conditional sale. That means you could get him out in 90 days—sooner if you hire a good real estate lawyer."

"What about getting paid earlier—" (he took a booklet out of his pocket and did some calculating) "—than 30 years?"

"I think he'll go for a balloon payment in 15 years."

"Well, George, you've plugged all the holes. I guess meeting the buyer ought to be the next step. Let's see if he's as good as you say."

I shored up Lowell with a few more arguments.

"I know you're overpaying for the property," I said, "but as I told you, the 5 per cent interest more than makes up for it. But there's another advantage. You can take depreciation on the basis of $6,600,000 less the land and that's worth a lot of money. However, I want to caution you. Don't take my word for it. Check with your attorney, or better still, with the Internal Revenue Service, as to whether the low interest rate will impinge on the depreciation allowance. It shouldn't, but play it safe."

"This suggests another problem," Lowell mused. "Won't the real estate assessor be influenced by the higher sales price and raise the tax assessment?"

"You raise an interesting point. However, you can point out to the assessor that the low down payment, 5 per cent interest and land contract sale, ought to preclude it from being regarded as a conventional sale. Your strongest argument is that on a cash sale which would require third party 10 per cent financing, the center would never sell for more than the assessed $4,500,000. In fact, you could produce evidence from the seller that he tried to sell it for $5,000,000, and couldn't.

"You'll admit," Lowell said, "that these factors are potential negatives. They could affect my depreciation and cash flow."

"I agree. However, to offset them, let me point out three positives. First, the percentage rents of the key tenants have been increasing about $10,000 a year since the center opened twelve years ago; second, low rent leases are expiring in a few years and there's room to jack them up about $50,000 a year; and third, there's land to expand the center another 50,000 square feet. When you add up all the positives and negatives, you've still got a darned good deal."

When Lowell and John finally met, they hit it off beautifully. After several meetings, each brought in his lawyer, and the contracts were drawn. Except for changing a few details, the hard-core terms remained—the price $6,600,000, the interest 5 per cent. Even my commission was agreed upon—$100,000 to be paid at the rate of $10,000 a year.

A few days before signing, John called.

"George, I've hit a snag. The heirs of the other two-thirds ownership had a change of heart. They approved of my negotiations all along, until a few days ago. I don't know what happened, but they want to wait."

"Needless to say, I'm deeply disappointed."

"Not as much as I am. I had visions of being a free man. I even planned a trip abroad. Now I'm harnessed again, and I don't like it. But what can I do? I'm the only one who knows how to run the center. The heirs of the other two-thirds are widows and inexperienced. All I can say is, let's wait and see."

My buyer was more disappointed than both of us. His visions of going out on his own and making the center hum were blasted.

And so was my conduit theory. John, Lowell and I are waiting. So far, there's no better plan to break the management impasse than the conduit idea which I had so diligently worked out, and which was only a few days from being consummated.

I don't consider this a defeat—only a part of an educational process.

UPPING THE PRICE AND LOWERING THE INTEREST SELLS A SCHOOL

My failure to sell the $6,600,000 shopping center resulted in success elsewhere. It triggered an idea in the mind of the attorney who represented the seller in the aborted negotiations.

He had been trying for several months to buy a building for a religious school. The seller was the owner of an art school that was going out of business. The attorney, who was president of the religious school, was authorized by his board of directors not to pay more than $1,000,000 with a $300,000 down payment and the balance at the current 10 per cent interest rate on a 20 year amortization, or about $90,000 a year. The art company insisted on its $1,500,000 price and the deal stalled—even though the seller was anxious to get rid of the vacant buildings, and the religious school could make good use of them. When the attorney saw how close his seller and my buyer had come to making an over-priced deal on the shopping center, he decided to try the same approach to break the price barrier on the school. His board of directors authorized him to offer $1,500,000 with $300,000 down, provided the balance of $1,200,000 could be paid off at the rate of about $90,000 a year, to include interest and principal, interest at 5 per cent. It was the same deal in different clothing.

The board of directors of the art company wrestled with the offer for several weeks and finally accepted it. They were knowledgeable enough to know that by cutting the interest rate, they were cutting the price, but I believe two factors persuaded them to take it. One was psychological—they got their price. The other was financial—if the interest rate dropped, they would in effect be getting close to their price. At any rate, the deal was made.

I was glad to see my theory of equity financing work. The kicker of higher price balancing off lower interest rate, was receiving practical acceptance. The religious school has moved into the premises and the art school is getting its monthly checks regularly. Backed by the religious community, the buyer will prove to be an excellent conduit for the remaining $1,200,000.

The educative process is working. Mark my word! The conduit idea, with its corollaries of higher prices and lower interest rates as a way to free capital, will avalanche into a torrent of new deals. It's one of the most effective ways to counter the insurmountable costs of exorbitant third-party financing.

USING THE CONDUIT METHOD ON THE SALE OF A GOLF COURSE

Pat's real estate problem was tailor-made for the conduit method. He built a beautiful 27-hole golf course in 1964, and finding it difficult to manage, leased it for ten years at about $75,000 a year based on a disadvantageous percentage formula. He owed $1,250,000 at 6 per cent when he finished it, but the interest rate kept rising (the lender had an open-ended interest rate), until in 1974 he was paying 10 per cent.

Pat was furious. This was one of the few times it paid to get angry. He owned a big block of stock which he bought for a song, and which was now selling at $90 a share. He sold $1,250,000 worth, walked into the savings-and-loan office, laid a certified check on the table, and said:

"Here's your money. I'll be damned before I'll pay your usurious 10 per cent rate."

The stock is now selling at $10 a share. Pat got mad at the right time.

But he had a problem. The golf course with its beautiful clubhouse and olympic swimming pool now cost him $2,000,000. He had shown a loss of about $60,000 a year during the lease period. Now the lease was terminating, and at 68, he was faced with running the golf course at a time when he was planning to retire.

Several months before the expiration of the lease, I asked Pat; "What are you going to do with the golf course now?"

"Sell it," he said decisively.

"For how much?"

"For what I've got in it—$2,000,000."

After talking to him for a while, I delineated these facts: The net income from 300 members at $500 a year was about $150,000; the net income from outside golf outings, about $100,000; the net earnings from $500,000 of food and liquor, about $50,000—a total of $300,000. The general expenses were about $100,000 a year for the maintenance of the golf course and clubhouse; $50,000 for real estate taxes; and about $25,000 for miscellaneous. That left a net of about $125,000 a year before debt service.

When I digested the projected operating statement, I asked:

"How can you justify a $2,000,000 price?"

"First," he said, "that's what it cost me. Second, it would take $3,000,000 to reproduce it. And third, that's what I want, period."

"But be reasonable, Pat. At today's interest rates, it would require $250,000 to amortize $2,000,000 at 10 per cent. The buyer would have to lose $125,000 a year to buy your place. It doesn't make sense."

"That's his problem," he said crustily.

But it was Pat's problem more than the buyer's. He had been trying to sell for a year with zero results.

"Pat," I said firmly, "I know you can afford to be cocky because you own it free and clear, but in a few months you'll have to run the place. Do you want the headaches at your age?"

"I have no choice."

"But you have."

"What choice?"

I went into a long dissertation on the practicability of the conduit method, and how much better off he would be selling it that way than running the golf course himself. He listened attentively, then asked:

"All right. You've told me how you structured and muffed the shopping-center deal, and how the attorney put together the religious-school deal, now tell me how you'd structure mine."

"The logical way to start is with the net after all expenses before debt service. It's $125,000 a year. That's point number one. No one is going to buy it and pay more than that on debt service. If he does, he'll have negative cash flow. He'll lose money."

"What's point number two?" Pat asked, not too encouragingly.

"To get a durable conduit who will have youth and managerial ability to act as a responsible pipeline to pass through the money from the golf course to you."

"How much money?"

"That's point number three, but no more important than the other two. $2,100,000 is a price that's fair to you and one the buyer can live with, providing—listen carefully, these are crucial points—providing that the down payment is no more than $200,000, the interest rate 5 per cent, and the debt service $125,000 a year."

I looked at Pat's face. At first, it was neutrally absorbing the figures, then his expression changed to one of confrontation.

"It would take about 30 years before my estate would get its money."

"What's wrong with a $125,000 annuity for 30 years?"

"It's better at $250,000 a year. I don't want to stretch the payments so long."

"But anyone agreeing to that would not know what he's doing. It would be a prescription for default. You wouldn't want a guy like that."

"But if he increased the 300 membership to 500, he could pay the $250,000."

"And have nothing left for himself. He'd still be a fool. I agree the membership can be increased, but that's my ace-in-the-hole argument for getting my buyer to agree on the terms I've outlined. That's when I can say that adding another 200 new members gets you $100,000 profit. That's the exciting part of the deal for the buyer—the potential. Take that away and you have no deal. Remember, his layer of profit protects your $125,000-a-year cash flow. Remove his potential and you remove his incentive. That's the rational way to look at this deal—not the way you've been doing—closing your eyes and blindly asking $2,000,000 cash."

"You're awfully convincing. Do you have any particular conduit in mind?"

"Not yet. But if you think I make sense, I'll produce one."

"Go ahead."

For several weeks I tried to think of a young man who would fit into the golf-course picture. None came to mind. Then one day while playing Pat's golf course with a Realtor who was outscoring me on almost every hole, I casually happened to mention that the golf course was for sale.

"You know," he said, "I'd chuck in my real estate business if I could figure out a way to buy it."

"Do you really mean that?" I asked. "Are you serious?"

He was a man in his early forties who did a creditable job selling commercial real estate on the three days a week that he wasn't playing golf. The game was his first love—money, second.

"In the back of my mind I have always had a yen for running a golf course," he said thoughtfully. "I think it's a great way to make a living—and have fun."

My chance remark flushed out a serious prospect. Very often small incidents start big deals. It did in this case.

In the locker room after the game, he over a Scotch and soda and I over a ginger ale on the rocks, began a serious discussion on how to purchase the golf course. After I explained the conduit method and projected the gross income and net cash flow, I told him about Pat's interest in a $2,100,000 price with $200,000 down and $125,000 yearly payments at 5 per cent interest. I then capped my explanation with this clinching argument:

"All you have to do is sell another 200 memberships at $500 apiece and you've got a $100,000 yearly profit. It's not going to be easy, but with your knowledge of the local golf world, it may not be so difficult."

"There's only one thing that bothers me about this deal."

"What's that?"

"The high price. I know he couldn't get much more than a million cash for it, yet you want me to pay $2,100,000. How do I reconcile myself to it?"

"By telling yourself that you're saving a million dollars in interest—the difference between 5 and 10 per cent."

"It's an ingenious way to construct a deal," he said. "Highly unorthodox. Let me think about it."

A few days later he called.

"I'm interested. I'd like to meet the seller."

Three months before the ten year lease on the golf course was to expire, they met and ironed out most of the details, leaving the hard-core terms of price, down payment, interest rate, and yearly payment to remain as I constructed it. I drew the contract.

A few days before signing, Pat called and said apologetically:

"George, I just can't go through with it, and I can't give you a good reason. Your deal makes sense in one way, and confuses me in another. I'm going to make another stab at getting $2,000,000 cash. If I fail, I promise to get back to you."

"What are you going to do in the meantime?"

"Run the course myself. I know it sounds crazy, but I've no choice."

He's been doing it for a year now, spending half his time operating the golf course, and the other half trying to sell it for $2,000,000 cash.

In the meantime, my buyer is waiting, waiting until the elderly owner wakes up to the practical logic of my conduit theory.

THE CONDUIT CONCEPT OFFERS A LOGICAL SOLUTION TO A PERPLEXING REAL ESTATE PROBLEM

The four-story, 40,000 square-foot Babcock Bank Building was the jewel of Third Street. It was the hub of a business area that was second in importance only to Milwaukee's metropolitan downtown. But that was 40 years ago.

Since then the area has slid downhill, and a former salesman of mine who owned the bank building was now struggling to keep it economically afloat.

One day, Fred, the owner, phoned me.

"When I worked for you, unraveling problem deals was always one of your challenging enjoyments. Well, I've got a dandy for you. Would you mind brainstorming it with me?"

"O.K.," I said, "What's the problem?"

"In a nutshell, I've been groping with the Babcock Building for five years, and I still can't see daylight. I've been averaging 50 per cent occupancy and grossing $35,000 a year. I have no mortgage on it, yet my fixed expenses of $25,000 leave me only $10,000 a year. And that, with a lot of huffing-and-puffing management. What do I do? I can't sell it—I've tried. I don't want to own it—I'm tired. I'm getting on in years and management has become a hassle. I'm at my wit's end. A free and clear building that would cost over a million to reproduce, yet it's causing me all kinds of headaches."

Luckily for him, I happened to have had a meeting with the director of the Urban League several days ago. I carried away a picture of makeshift and congested offices. As Fred was talking, my mind was working.

"Fred," I said enthusiastically, "I think I have the answer." I stopped for a moment to pull my thoughts together. "Listen carefully, and follow me step by step. Go and see the director of the Urban League and present him with the following proposition—a deal he can't refuse—it's that good."

"Good for him or me?"

"For both. Listen. Set a price of $125,000 for the Babcock Building and $25,000 for the Urban League Building. Agree to take their building as a down payment on yours with the balance of $100,000 to be paid at the rate of $10,000 a year without interest. Now, let me tell you why it's a good deal for you. I know, and you know, you couldn't get $75,000 for your building in cash. There's simply no market for it. My plan is good for you because the Urban League becomes a reliable conduit through which you get a steady $10,000 yearly annuity for ten years—an amount you can't bank on in the future as the owner. And you might sell the present Urban League property on a land contract with a small down payment for another $25,000.

"Now let's see if it's a good deal for the Urban League," I continued. "The League moves out of its congested old quarters into the 20,000 vacant square feet of the Babcock Building. And it has a better chance of holding on to the $35,000-a-year rent you're now getting because many of the tenants are related agencies. Since the fixed expenses on your building are about $25,000 a year, the League could use the $10,000 net to pay off the $100,000 balance at my suggested $10,000 a year. That amounts to getting 20,000 square feet in the Babcock Building free, and paying off the mortgage at the same time. And they would be occupying space five times as good, twice as large and in a better neighborhood. How could they refuse a deal like that?"

"I think it's an excellent plan. And I can't think of anyone who could put my building to better use than the Urban League. I'm grateful, George. I'm going to test your idea the first thing tomorrow morning."

I called Fred several weeks later to see how he was doing.

Not good, and I can't understand it. Either I didn't present it right, or they were afraid of the responsibility of owning a big building. Whatever the reason, I still have my headaches and the Urban League is still burdened with congestion."

"Don't be discouraged," I said. "Sometimes an innovative idea takes time to jell. Be patient. Wait. I wouldn't be surprised if in a few months they call asking if the deal is still available."

* * *

As a footnote to this chapter, let me suggest that I see no other
viable alternatives to the sale of the shopping center, golf course or
Babcock Building than the ways I've suggested. Eventually the
resistances will yield to the realities of the sellers' and buyers' needs.
The sellers will have to make their moves, and the deals will be made.
Unwillingness will inevitably yield to prudence.

SUMMARY OF THE CONDUIT IDEA

Here is a step-by-step approach to developing and consummating a deal that will produce a dependable yearly income using
the conduit technique.

1. Find an elderly owner who is either mismanaging his
property, or is getting tired of it, and is looking to trade in his
managerial problems for a care-free annual income.

2. You can find such an owner by asking questions—at
meetings, cocktail parties, or calling friends and owners directly.
You'll be amazed at the leads you'll uncover when you launch on an
imaginative search.

3. When you find a likely candidate, be sure you explain your
conduit plan clearly and thoroughly, citing the advantages and
disadvantages. Be honest. Tell him the main disadvantage is that
you're taking control of his property with only seed money, and that if
you can't produce, he's likely to have his property back in his lap—
probably in worse economic condition than when he sold it to you.

4. It's at this point that you'll either make or break your deal. If
you can't point to any character assets or skills in managing real
estate to counteract his fears, don't blame him for blowing the deal.
Blame yourself.

5. You have no right to expect someone to turn over a million
dollars worth of property, with let's say $50,000 down, if you haven't
taken any courses in property management or can't point to a record
of dependability and stability in other areas of your life.

3

How to Risk Prudently

Risking is an art which requires prudence, strong nerves and wisdom—wisdom being the most important. Without wisdom it's easy to lose perspective, and that's when ambition can run you into trouble. With wisdom you see more clearly and limit the dangers. Let me show you what I mean.

TIMIDITY COST MY FRIEND $250,000

An overly ambitious developer, thinking the 1970's would be a duplication of the affluent 1960's, built simultaneously on speculation a 100,000 square foot industrial building, several large apartment projects and 120 condominiums. In 1973 the tight money coils began encircling him, and in 1974 its tentacles squeezed all the cash out of him. He was left gasping for money when little of it was available. That's when he asked me to help him cash out the remaining 50 unsold units of his 120-condominium project.

Here indeed, was a great opportunity for someone in a high income bracket to make a lot of money. Here's the way the deal stacked up....

Jaren, the wheeling-dealing owner, owed $700,000 in interim financing on the remaining 50 condos at 12 per cent interest. It was due, together with about $50,000 in delinquent interest. In addition, Jaren had not paid a year's real estate taxes of $40,000, and he was five months behind on the $40-a-month upkeep per condominium, for a total of $10,000. His total arrearage was $800,000 with the expenses on the unsold 50 units running at the monthly rate of $7,000 in interest, $4,000 in real estate taxes, $2,000 for maintenance, or a total of $13,000 a month.

A few additional facts before getting at the solution. Jaren sold the 70 units at an average price of $27,500. The project was well conceived and well built. Each condominium had a good sized living room, dinette, kitchen, two bedrooms and two baths—a total of 1,200 square feet—semi-luxury construction. The special amenities were elaborate—an acre of gardens and an olympic size swimming pool, a beautiful recreation room for tenant parties featuring a large woodburning fireplace, separate saunas for men and women, indoor parking for owners and ample outside parking for guests. It was a good, middle-class location, and fortunately the first 70 owners included a sprinkling of attorneys, judges, policemen, and teachers to give it a stable base.

To ease the burden, Jaren rented ten of the condominiums at $275 a month. He could easily have rented more. But that would not have solved his problem. The lender wanted cash, not rented condominiums.

Now for the solution! 1974 was a good year for the gasoline business. Harold, a friend of mine who owned 30 gasoline stations, was making $300,000 a year and prodding me to get him into a good real estate deal. I suggested that he buy the 50 condominiums from Jaren on the following terms:

Harold should pay the $50,000 arrearage in interest, $40,000 in real estate taxes, and $10,000 in maintenance, and give Jaren $25,000 for his equity, providing I could arrange with the mortgagee to extend the $700,000 interim mortgage for another year with no personal liability beyond paying 12 per cent interest for one year. In addition, Harold was to be responsible for a year's maintenance of about $25,000 and another $40,000 in real estate taxes. Harold's maximum exposure would then be about $275,000 if he didn't sell any condominiums. If you take a moment to add it up, you'll see I'm right. Since he was in the 50 per cent bracket, his total exposure would be about $137,500.

Now let's analyze the potential profit for taking this $137,500 maximum risk. I suggested to Harold that to speed up the sales, he could afford to slash the price from $27,500 to $24,000. I proposed a series of ads featuring pictures and statements from buyers saying: "Here are the reasons why I bought my condominium at Braun Port," and listing all the special amenities. A series of such ads, quoting some of the more prominent people who lived in the project, would have brought a good response.

With building in 1974 almost at a standstill and the cost to reproduce these new condominiums running at about $32,500 apiece, the chances of selling at least 40 of them within a year at $24,000 were better than good—they were excellent. Assuming $2,000 apiece for selling costs, my buyer could conceivably end up with 40 times $22,000 or $880,000. He'd then have enough to pay the $700,000 mortgage balance and have $180,000 from which to recoup his original $125,000 investment. That would still leave him $55,000 for current interest, real estate taxes and maintenance. With another $25,000 of his own money, he could probably end up owning ten of the rented condominiums free and clear.

Harold could then have the luxury of having the option of keeping them as an investment or leisurely selling them at $27,500 apiece and make a profit of about $250,000. This was my projected outline of the deal.

I considered it a prudent risk. Unfortunately, Harold did not. He was too timid. He put too much stress on the uncertainties of the times and not enough on the law of supply and demand. New construction was at a low ebb. That's what minimized the risk. But Harold didn't think so.

Another company read the signs correctly and bought the condominiums at approximately the terms I outlined. To satisfy my curiosity, I followed the deal closely. By November 1975, all the condominiums were sold at $25,000 apiece.

HOW I EVALUATED THE RISK
WHEN I DECIDED TO BUILD THE FIRST MODERN,
AIR-CONDITIONED OFFICE BUILDING IN OUR CITY

Here's a description of the biggest gamble of my life.

In 1956, I decided to build the first modern, centrally air-conditioned office building in Milwaukee. Why? Because I thought it was a prudent risk and that it would make an excellent investment.

Let's analyze the pros and cons as they existed at the time. The process of arraying the pluses against the minuses is a valuable preliminary in delineating the risk elements of a prospective project. First, what were the pluses? Other cities of Milwaukee's size were building modern office buildings and leasing them as soon as they came on the market. Denver was a prime example. In 1957 when I attended a Building Owners and Managers conference, I noted that two large new office buildings were completed and filled at $5 a square foot. "Why doesn't someone build a new office building in this town?" some of the executives of national firms would ask me at business luncheons. First-grade office space at the time was bringing $3 a square foot and second-grade space about $2 a square foot. Would tenants pay $5 for new space? "Yes," was their unanimous answer. That was plus number one.

Parking was becoming an acute problem. Offices and parking were often separated by two or three blocks; undercover parking ajacent to new office space would be an innovative amenity prospective tenants would value highly. That would be plus number two. And quiet, central, air conditioning instead of noisy window boxes; acoustical ceilings with flush fluorescent lighting instead of bleak incandescent lamps; and offices partitioned to needs instead of poor layouts wasting space, could be pluses number three, four and five. There were many favorable factors. And the timing was right—there was no competition.

But was I ready for such a big undertaking? I had little experience in leasing prime office space—that was a definite minus. Then, there was the question of how big to build it; 50,000 square feet? That wouldn't be monumental enough to attract the big-name tenants like Prudential, General Motors, Mutual of New York, etc. But I dared not build it too big either—there was the danger of overreaching the office-space demand and decreasing my chances of financing it.

Assuming now that the demand was there, that the time was ripe, and the size was right—wasn't this project something for a national firm with a lot of financial staying power, instead of a single entrepreneur with limited equity ($300,000) although unlimited hope and confidence? It was a minus that rankled in my mind, but not enough to stop me.

I decided on a seven-story office building of 200,000 square feet and an adjacent 450-car parking garage. But there wasn't a square block available in the down-town area, and if there was, the high cost would wipe out all my hopes anyway. So I bought a 250 x 400 foot site two miles away from down-town for $175,000, and squirmed in indecision as I wondered whether tenants would be willing to move away from their traditional down-town locations.

Even after I bought the lot, I still hesitated. I interviewed dozens of prospective tenants about my out-of-the-way location, about the $5 per square foot rate and about the special amenities I had to offer. I weighed the positive and negative responses, and the positive ones predominated.

Of course, I was plagued with the problem of financing. Do I sell office space from plans, so I can offer the lender signed leases to help my financing; or do I obtain permanent financing first, so that I can induce tenants to sign leases, knowing they'll have a building to move into? It was a case of which came first, the chicken or the egg. Having carefully analyzed all the pluses and minuses, I took a deep breath and plunged into the biggest gamble I had ever taken. I came out with the biggest, single, self-created yearly income of my real estate career—$165,000 cash flow after all fixed expenses and payments on a $2,800,000 mortgage—with less than $300,000 seed money. It's a stupefying figure when you realize that it would have taken two lifetimes of $50,000-a-year earnings, invested after paying taxes, to earn $165,000 a year. I did it in 18 months. It's incredible. But that's how building a yearly income accelerates when you use the revolutionary method of creating your own projects.

With it came the biggest reward of all—an opportunity to be creative and meet the needs of people. Without that philosophical perspective, real estate activity inevitably degenerates into aimless excitement.

A DEAL WHERE "HEADS I WIN, AND TAILS I CAN'T LOSE"

Joe, an alert young man, read a news story about a halfway house idea that involved taking trusted prisoners out of jail and allowing them to live in a dormitory prior to their release. The story suggested that the state might try it out for a two-year period, and if it worked, the plan would be continued.

Joe followed the developments closely and six months later when the state agency was ready, he was ready too—with an old mansion which he bought for $15,000, and which lent itself to remodeling for housing 45 inmates. While others looked at the deal for the first time, Joe had already ascertained that the remodeling costs for such a facility would be $45,000.

He offered to lease the remodeled building to the state for $30,000 a year net for two years. This was attractive to the state because it had no obligations to continue beyond the two years, and a no-lose deal for Joe, because if the state moved out, he would lose no money—he'd have a free and clear remodeled building. The $60,000 rent would pay for the building and remodeling. But Joe figured he'd do a lot better than be left with a vacant building at the end of two years. Then when the state agency renewed the lease, his no-lose gamble would really pay off.

Sure enough. When the two-year lease expired, the agency was so satisfied with the results of the halfway house, and with the way Joe remodeled the property, that it entered into a new five-year lease at the rate of $27,500 a year with a proviso that Joe spend another $15,000 for a few more amenities. The State saved money by transferring inmates from a high cost, high-security prison, to a low cost, low-security halfway house; and Joe built a good-sized yearly income helping it do it.

Let's not begrudge Joe this easily earned money. He looked at twenty old buildings before he found one that was big enough, in the right neighborhood, and didn't require exorbitant remodeling costs. Had the state not renewed the lease, it would have been an ordinary, prudent deal—a lot of work for ordinary results. But he was willing to risk his time (where others did not), thus positioning himself for an extraordinary five-year income bonanza. This deal is an example of a prudent real estate adage—if you maximize alertness, you minimize risk.

A REAL ESTATE DEAL WITH LOW RISK, HIGH PROFITS, AND BENEFITS TO THE NEEDY

Those who quip that, "Money isn't everything—only 99 per cent," are a cynical lot. And I might add that those who make a game out of making money and don't enjoy the wholesome feeling that making a contribution to society gives, are settling for peanuts. They settle for raucous excitement and rarely experience the still joy of a caring attitude.

This leads me naturally into Section 8 of subsidized housing, where you can make a substantial contribution to the housing of the needy by investing your time and very little money. But the rewards are big for those who are looking to build a yearly income, and especially profitable for those in a high income bracket. It's one of the most creative partnerships between public and private enterprise to shore up our sagging housing economy.

To motivate builders to satisfy the high demand for low-income housing, the federal government is offering these carrots: (1) Only 2 per cent equity requirement; (2) Interim interest, real estate taxes, and miscellaneous losses during construction to shelter high-income investors; (3) The builder's option to sell these benefits for cash.

Let's take a typical Section 8, one million dollar housing project, consisting of 60 one- and two-bedroom apartments. Let's assume that the physical improvements exclusive of land are $900,000. The Federal Housing Administration allows 10 per cent of the $900,000 for builders' work and makes it an allowable cost of the project. Thus, the cost components of the project could be $900,000 for improvements, $90,000 for the builder's fee for putting it in place, and let's say $70,000 for land, for a total of $1,060,000. The 90 per cent mortgage would then be about $1,040,000, and the 2 per cent builder's equity about $20,000.

A few additional details. The builder is allowed a 6 per cent return on the $90,000 and $20,000, or a total of $110,000 for a yearly yield of $6,600. He is also allowed a management fee of 5 or 6 per cent of the gross rent, or whatever the local management fee happens to be.

After the builder obtains the mortgage, either conventionally or FHA insured, and the Federal Government approves the builder's cost figures, as well as the rentals of let's say, $185 for a one-bedroom apartment and $235 for a two-bedroom apartment, it will then guarantee to pay the difference every month between the allowable rents of $185 and $235, and what the qualified needy tenants can afford to pay. If according to a government formula, which calls for a tenant to pay no more than one-fifth of his monthly earnings for monthly rent, a one-bedroom qualifier is $60 short, or a two-bedroom qualifier is $70 short, then the government will send these checks monthly to the builder, so he can keep his project in the black.

For those who are not interested in the 6 per cent return and 5 per cent management fee, there's another way to benefit from Section 8 Subsidized Housing.

The interest cost for interim financing during construction for a million-dollar project could be from $75,000 to $100,000, depending upon the interest rate and length of the building period. The real estate taxes levied during construction could be about $20,000. Then there are other miscellaneous fees which are a one-time cost, and deductible. That could be another $5,000. And then there are "points"—the fee the lender charges to make an FHA loan whose interest rate might be lower than that of a conventional loan. All these are tax deductible in the year they occur. On a million-dollar project, they could be as high as $150,000. And during the next seven years you are likely to have another $200,000 of losses which can be used as offsets against ordinary gains. These losses are saleable to limited partners in high income brackets. The builder can remain the general partner and keep this 6 per cent return and management fee. And he can sell 98 per cent of the project together with the $150,000 construction losses and $200,000 of future accelerated depreciation for as high as $150,000 in cash. The builder must make sure that the buyer is in the picture before construction begins, so the purchaser can take the accelerated depreciation as a first owner. I suggest that you hire a good lawyer who is familiar with all the legal implications of subsidized housing. I'm only giving you a skeleton idea; it's up to you to flesh it out with his help and that of government bureaucrats.

One day, a builder invited me to visit his 80 unit, subsidized rental project. As he was showing me through the well-lighted corridors and some of the plain but handsome apartments, I saw at firsthand the glowing gratefulness of the tenants.

"God bless you for making it possible for me to live here," an elderly woman said to my host as we stopped at her open door.

Another lady who proudly showed us through her rooms, kissed the owner as he was leaving. "You'll never know how happy you've made me," she effused.

Before we were through inspecting the apartments, the owner received more "God bless you's" than others get in a lifetime.

"I have a pretty good idea what you stand to gain financially from this project," I said as we were walking to our cars, "but I see something more. These tenants are truly grateful. You know, in some ways you're giving them more therapy than their doctors and ministers. They're living in spanking new apartments which, but for you and the government, they could never afford or enjoy."

"It's a reward," he said modestly, "I didn't expect."

There isn't a prudent risk I can recommend more highly than building under Section 8. The risk is miniscule and the rewards are great—profitable and contributory.

THE SCENARIO OF A PRUDENT DEAL

I'm flirting with one of the most revolutionary deals I've ever attempted. I'm thinking of converting a 10 story, 150,000 square foot, downtown furniture store into 100 little shops with living quarters to the rear. I believe it's a prudent project.

The general concept is to divide each of the ten floors (100 X 150) with a 20 foot wide mall, leaving a depth of approximately 40 feet on each side for some sort of shop in front with live-in area to the rear. Thus, a barber, a music teacher, a jeweler, etc., could have the rent for his shop and living quarters cut in half, or perhaps less than half. I intend to lease a 1,000 square foot area for about $300 a month, or about $3.50 a square foot. That ought to provide enough room for a small store and living space for one or two people. Of course, prospective tenants would be able to lease larger areas if they desire. Given proper advertising, an outdoor and indoor directory, and unusual shops, the tenants could benefit from the traffic generated by two nearby banks, a dozen office buildings and a major department store.

So far so good. But here are a few problems. The area is not zoned for residential use. And our city code reads that an owner must provide a parking stall for each residential unit. The furniture building has no parking. That, among other reasons, is why it can be bought for $275,000 or less!

At night strangers stalk the area around the building. Nearby, other vacant buildings add to the ominous silence. There are no people living for blocks around. That's the trouble with our downtowns. They're used noisily during the day and are deserted at night. Our downtowns have been planned for buildings, not for people.

Using a bit of unusual real estate philosophy, I intend to ask the city fathers to give me a zoning variance for the residential use of the furniture building, and to eliminate the parking requirement. There are several public parking garages nearby that are half-filled during the day and empty at night. That ought to take care of my parking problem.

Several city officials look kindly at my idea, but our codes are strict and it'll take a lot of doing to get the concessions I need to make this a viable project. And, of course, there's always the risk—will people want to live downtown? I think they will, because the low rents will be a great incentive.

Here's the way the project stacks up financially:

COST

1.	Purchase price (hopefully)	$200,000
2.	120 baths & kitchens @ $2,000	240,000
3.	15,000 lineal feet of partitions @ $15 a foot	225,000
4.	Electric	65,000
5.	Heat	70,000
6.	Construct malls, paint, outdoor treatment & miscellaneous	100,000
7.	Interest and taxes during construction	100,000
		$1,000,000

INCOME

	100 apartments and shops at $3,500	$350,000 a
1.	Debt service on $1,200,000 at 9 1/2%, 30 yr. amortization about	$125,000 a
2.	Fixed expenses (listed below)	130,000 a
3.	TOTAL	$235,000
	Cash flow before vacancies	$ 95,000 a

EXPENSES

Real estate taxes	$ 40,000
Heat	25,000
Light	15,000
Repairs	10,000

Miscellaneous	15,000
Janitor	10,000
Management	15,000
TOTAL	$130,000

If the city would go along with my variance requests, I'd be tempted to risk going into this deal for several reasons. As the figures show, it's not a bad investment. But more fascinating is the chance to start something new and revolutionary going downtown. Within one square mile of the furniture building there are about a dozen vacant structures gathering dust and losing money for the owners. What a contribution I could make if my efforts could create the momentum toward building a new downtown village out of old buildings. I'd feel a glow of accomplishment if I could see the tenants walk the streets at night saying "hi" to one another, instead of looking at the deserted ghost area it is today. That's why I think the furniture building conversion would be a prudent investment, indeed.

TEN PRINCIPLES OF PRUDENT REAL ESTATE INVESTING

1. *Location.* There is a popular real estate axiom that the three most important features of any deal are location, location, and location. There is more truth in this than exaggeration. I'd like to strengthen its importance by adding this: in appraising location, it's not enough to evaluate its present—you should also project its future. The facts and insights you bring to bear in assessing a location will help you to determine the feasibility and stability of a real estate investment.

2. *Know yourself!* It's one of the wisest philosophical imperatives. Translated on the firing line of action, it means don't bite off more than you can chew. It means don't go into a million-dollar deal before you've successfully handled a deal of a hundred-thousand dollars.

Different variables play on a $50,000 duplex, a $500,000 apartment complex, or a $5,000,000 shopping center. The bigger the deal, the more subtle and complicated it becomes. And the easier it is to make a mistake. Evaluate your capacity honestly. It is far wiser to stay within a $100,000 deal and succeed, than risk $500,000 and fail. Only you can judge where you belong.

3. *Financial limits.* Closely related to your capacity to handle complicated matters are your financial limitations. It's always safer to go into a deal where your talents are greater than the availability of money. It's fatal when it's the other way around—when the money needed exceeds your ability to handle it.

Don't be like one of my young readers who called from Memphis, Tennessee, one day, asking how he could skip the piddly deals and get into the big leagues right away. After talking to him awhile, I could tell he had neither the talent nor the money to handle anything but "piddly" deals. Over-reaching in either one or the other category is a prescription for failure.

4. *Is it feasible?* It's a question that creeps into every deal, and asks, simply, does it make sense? Some answer with feasibility studies, others by intuition—or in the vernacular, by the seat of their pants. I've seen deals smothered to death with expensive feasibility studies, and some that turned into outstanding failures after all feasibility reports said "go". I've also seen deals fail because developers used neither common sense nor factual information. The ideal combination is a wise mixture of intuition and fact, and as far as I'm concerned, the more intuition the better, because intuition presupposes an integration of common sense facts.

5. *Is it financeable?* Some deals are financeable and some are not. For instance, a skyscraper in Sheboygan, Wisconsin, a town of 46,000, would not be financeable, but a 12-family would. Or, if there is an overabundance of office space and apartments in a certain city, neither an office building nor an apartment project would be financeable.

Changing old buildings into new uses is financable if you can produce a pro forma operating statement showing its feasibility. But I'd like to warn you that this is a new field, and lenders, being naturally more conservative than developers, will look at your deal with a wary eye. However, if you can muster all the arguments described in Chapter 11 of this book in favor of the conversion of old buildings, you may be able to overcome the lender's reluctance.

6. *Is there a need for it?* This is crucial from a financial as well as a moral standpoint. A deal is not a good investment if it's not needed. An overabundance in homes, apartments, office buildings or shopping centers has bankrupted many a builder. Nor should you enter into a deal that's financially feasible but morally wrong. Does it pay to prostitute your character to meet the needs of massage parlor and gambling casino operators? I say no, even if the return is 100 per cent or more, because you're not meeting the legitimate needs of people. If you're only looking at a deal financially, and not at what it contributes to society, you're settling for peanuts. It may be smart, but it's not wise.

7. *Is there room for originality?* If you can possibly help it, don't settle for the usual—strive for the unusual—whether it's in building or in management. Look at the new kinds of real estate shelter that creative minds have produced during the last 25 years— shopping centers, housing for the elderly, industrial parks, condominiums. And what about special recreational amenities for tenants—tennis courts, swimming pools, saunas, libraries, meeting rooms and restaurants? The host-guest relationships that develop between landlord and tenant as a result of serving people better are not only commendable in themselves, but they turn good investments into excellent ones. The innovators not only made a lot of money, but they had a lot of fun. Who says that only artists, musicians, and writers experience the joys of creativity? Converting an oil-slicked automobile garage into small theaters, restaurants and shops, where young people can get a toehold in the Establishment, can make the creative juices flow as abundantly as painting a great masterpiece.

8. *Does the investment lend itself to cost cutting, rent increment, or both?* A poor investment can be turned into a good one if there is room for cutting expenses or raising rents. One of my students bought a 20-family apartment building that was bringing $38,000 a year rent. He spent $10,000 upgrading it, and raised the rent to $51,000, thus increasing its value by about $100,000 in one year.

I have seen many instances where expenses were decreased by 10 per cent when a buyer took personal charge of a building that was previously managed by remote control. Saving heat by installing timers, reducing electric wattage in public areas, getting repairs and painting done cheaper, and reducing real estate taxes where they're unusually high—all these and more can reduce operating expenses by thousands of dollars.

There are many deals where sellers understate expenses and overstate the income, making it a poor deal if you accept them at face value. There are also deals in poorly managed properties where the expenses are too high and rents too low, making it possible for an alert buyer to turn an ordinary deal into an extraordinary one.

9. *Do the financial terms of the deal give you breathing room?* This is very important. A friend of mine built a 40-room motel and foolishly agreed to pay off the $400,000 mortgage in 10 years. He "choked" himself on the terms. He was doing a fairly good business but the $50,000-a-year mortgage payments killed his investment. Had he gotten a 25-year loan with $30,000-a-year payments he could have made it. When foreclosure threatened, he sold out for a pittance.

In obtaining financing, do what the sophisticated borrowers do, thin out the payments to the limit. Get 30-year amortization, if you can, with the right to accelerate payments at your option. Don't strangle yourself with 10- or 15-year amortizations. They're deal killers.

10. *Should you sign personally?* That's a sticky question. If you make a bad deal, or when a good deal turns bad during bad times, you stand to lose not only your equity in the deal but some or all of your other assets. Yet, if you put it in a corporation, you lose valuable depreciation benefits. Or the lender may refuse to make the mortgage unless you sign personally. What to do?

If the lender won't let you off the hook, make him this proposition. Guarantee the top 15 or 20 per cent of the loan. That limits your exposure, and at the same time collateralizes the loan with an additional amount beyond your equity in the deal. I think this is fair and equitable to both lender and borrower.

AVOID THESE TEN MISTAKES

1. *Don't get into a deal involving eccentric and unreasonable tenants.* I've seen too many owners sell their apartment buildings at less than their worth because they couldn't manage obstinate tenants.

Know yourself. If you have a short fuse, don't buy a building with a long list of problems. Rather, make an investment with a net net lease, where the return is lower but free of management headaches.

2. *Don't get into a deal you can't control.* Too many get fleeced by taking a little piece of a big deal. The risk increases if the project is outside your own city. Don't rely on friends, they may know less than you do. And don't be mesmerized by high-powered salesmen who show you a beautiful rendering and then appeal to your vanity by inviting you to own a piece of it. Usually, a syndicated project is financed in ways you will not understand, and its operating statement, a guess at best, is usually puffed in favor of the promoter.

I'd rather see you buy a small building that you can manage, and use your own financial imagination, than rely on the financial machinations of others. Invest $10,000 innovatively in your own eight-family rather than in a fraction of a $10,000,000 deal. It's more fun that way, and usually more financially rewarding.

3. *As a starter, don't try to invest in commercial property.* You're safer with an apartment deal. Here are the reasons:

An office building, industrial property, or shopping center is a more volatile investment. If you're only 80 per cent occupied you're in trouble, and obtaining commercial tenants is a lot more difficult than finding residential ones. Unless you're unusually astute, try a few residential deals before stepping into the commercial ones. I know dozens of young men who did so well with residential properties that they found no need to seek out the riskier commercial deals. That's fine. There's no need to change if you're comfortable with what you're doing successfully.

4. *Don't pay all cash.* The astute investor sees the folly of buying a property for cash. There's no leverage in such a deal. The main economic advantage to look for in building an investment portfolio is property with a 12 per cent return against which you can borrow at a 9 to 10 per cent interest rate. When you pay all cash you limit yourself. When you can borrow 2 to 3 percentage points below the net rate of return of a property, you control more property with less of your own money.

A word of caution. Don't acquire more than you can adequately manage. Limit your acquisitions to your abilities. If management falters, then you're in trouble, especially if the interest rate becomes higher than the rate of return.

5. *Don't speculate in land.* It's too volatile an investment. Even the shrewdest get burnt. It's not for the neophyte. Yet, as stated

elsewhere in this book, when you take certain precautions and learn how to read the signs of the future, it does provide landfall op-portunities.

6. *Don't let ambition ride you.* Ambition, unrestrained by prudence, has caused many more bankruptcies than lack of knowledge or bad times. Foolish ambition blinds you, and binds you to a euphoric unreality. It mesmerizes you so that you listen to ap-plause rather than to your common sense. You grandstand for praise rather than see if your deals make economic sense.

When you get caught in the syndrome where all that matters is "show and dough", your efforts, like fireworks against a dark sky, may flare brilliantly one moment and die the next.

7. *Don't overpay.* I have seen investors so anxious to get into a deal, any deal, that they imprudently overlook the hazards and fall into a seller's trap. Investing is a cautious game—always stop, look, and listen to your common sense.

One of the common hazards is to fall in love with a building and lose your head in pride of ownership. Don't get stuck with a beautiful white elephant that barely produces a 5 per cent return when you can buy a prolific rabbit that keeps multiplying your investment.

Remember, $10,000 earned in an ordinary eight-family will buy as much as a $10,000 return from a luxurious four-family. Don't be impressed by monumental brick and mortar—but by the figures on the bottom line.

8. *Don't accept unreasonable terms.* Isn't it rather foolish to invest $10,000 and have nothing left after fixed expenses and debt service? You are not making a good deal unless you are getting the following:

(1) 10 per cent return on your investment after
     fixed expenses and debt service,
(2) about 1 per cent amortization,
(3) the advantage of depreciation,
(4) and a reasonable expectation of at least a 3 per
     cent rise in value every year due to inflation.

If the terms of your deal do not leave a 10 per cent cash-flow cushion, plus all the advantages mentioned above, you're not making a good investment. An astute buyer should enjoy a 15 per cent cushion after all expenses and amortization.

9. *Don't invest outside your community.* Unless there are unusual circumstances, you should not try to be an expert in someone else's back yard. Your chances of success in real estate investing decrease as you move away from your own community to other parts of the city, and they drop off drastically when you compete with the local experts in another city.

One of the reasons many of the public realty companies failed was because of the drubbing they received from the "local yokels", who were able to outmaneuver the public realty "slickers" because when the latter came to buy properties for their public portfolios, invariably the local owners knew more than the outsiders. When a New York, Chicago, or Los Angeles acquisition "expert" flew in for a day or two to buy an apartment project or office building in Peoria or Milwaukee, what chance did he have against the local talent? That's why outsiders lost millions in our city. They usually overpaid in their hurry to acquire properties for growth in their public companies. The local owners gladly accommodated them.

Don't make the same mistake. Invest close to home where you know as much about the local conditions as the next guy, so he doesn't take advantage of you nor you of him. Investing in your own community is not only a good investment principle, it's also good for your community.

10. *Don't invest in downtown property*—unless you can buy it for a song, or you have some unusual idea, like converting it into a mall or changing it into combination living quarters and shops.

There's little future for ordinary run-of-the-mill downtown property if it's held for ordinary use—like stores, second-rate office buildings, or multi-story loft structures. Their use is at the end of a cycle, and their trend is toward greater rather than smaller losses.

Unless there's an imaginative master design to beautify a downtown and make it more livable, there's little hope for a comeback. Most central cities are too far gone for any one individual to buck the trend. If you can see a plan formulating, fine—otherwise it's too hazardous an investment.

4

Profiles of Hazardous Real Estate Risks

The wildest gambler doesn't put all his chips on one roll of the dice. Risks should be taken in small gulps, so they can be digested. If a little deal gives you financial indigestion, at least you have a chance to analyze your mistakes, and with your reserves, try again.

The theory of going in for the kill is a foolish theory. It's as foolish as betting all you own on the Irish Sweepstakes. That's not the way to build an investment portfolio. That's a prescription for killing yourself financially.

ALL OR NOTHING IS NOT A PRUDENT RISK

Larry owned several small buildings which had a net income of $25,000 a year. He was a high-salaried advertising executive who made additional money in real estate and the stock market. He was reputed to be worth about a million dollars. One day he came to my office and said:

"George, I need some real estate excitement. Get me into some big deal with several small buildings I own as a down payment."

"What kind of property are you looking for?" I asked.

"Any kind, but it's got to be big."

71

Several months passed. Then something came to my attention. I called Larry.

"Still looking for that big deal?" I asked.

"I sure am," he answered cheerfully.

"I've got it for you."

"Great!"

"I have the 100,000 square foot Peerless Building in mind. I'm sure you know it well. The owner paid $1,100,000 for it several years ago, but he's now more interested in golf than in taking care of it. That's why it's only 75 per cent occupied. But even with the low occupancy, the gross rent is $365,000 a year. The fixed expenses are $200,000, leaving $165,000 net before debt service. I've got the owner to agree to sell it to you for $1,500,000 and allow you a credit of $200,000 for your properties. He further agrees to have the $1,300,000 balance payed off on the basis of $135,000 a year, including interest and principal, interest at 5 per cent. Let me add quickly that that's like paying less than $1,000,000 for the property if you had to pay the current rate of 10 per cent interest. Are you following me so far?"

"Go ahead."

"Here's why I think you should trade, if you're looking for an exciting deal. First, instead of being limited to a ceiling of $25,000 a year on your present properties, you have a potential of $30,000 a year cash flow after subtracting the $200,000 fixed expenses and the $135,000 yearly payment from the $365,000 gross rent. But that's just the beginning. You're well known in the city. If you let your executive friends know that you have 25,000 square feet to rent, you're bound to get some good leads. If you're successful in renting 20,000 square feet of it at say $3 a foot, you've got another $60,000. That's $90,000 instead of $25,000. Does that sound exciting?"

"Go on," he said thoughtfully.

'There are two hurdles before we can make the deal."

"What are they?"

"The owner of the Peerless Building doesn't want your properties in lieu of a $200,000 down payment. He wants cash."

"How do we handle that?"

"I've already handled it. I've called several investors to look at your properties and one of them is willing to pay $200,000 for them. The owner will now take your properties in trade for $200,000 since he has a take out, that is, someone who will buy them simultaneously with the sale of his building. Tax wise, the seller is in the same position, but you gain if your properties cost you less than $200,000. Are you following me?"

"All right, you've hurdled number one. What's the second hurdle?"

"He wants personal liability."

"Explain please."

"He wants you to personally guarantee the $135,000 a year payments."

"For how long?"

"For eight years."

"Too long."

"I agree. I've already negotiated it down to three years. He went along with me because he thinks you're a good risk. He's heard about you, and he likes what he's heard."

After half an hour of going over the deal point by point, he said:

"O.K. I'm interested. Let's go through the building sometime next week. And bring along a certified statement of operations."

After a month of negotiating, I could tell he was beginning to cool. When I asked him if there was anything wrong, he said:

"No, it looks like a pretty safe deal, but to be honest with you, I'm onto something really big. Nothing wrong with the deal or you, mind you. You're a persuasive fellow."

But, unfortunately for him, I wasn't persuasive enough. Some big wheeler-dealer got a hold of Larry and whipped his interest to a froth. He involved him in a $75,000,000 rental project on the West Coast that excited Larry out of his mind. Instead of taking a limited partnership position with limited income and limited personal liability, he was talked into taking a general partner's position with personal liability for his proportionate share of several million dollars. If the project went over, he could quadruple his investment of $300,000—if it failed, he stood to lose everything he owned.

Well, it was 1974, a bad year for real estate and the $75,000,000 big deal ran into big trouble. There were cost overruns, interim interest rates skyrocketed, and renting ground to a halt. As the project began to collapse financially, the lenders went after the general partners. Larry didn't grasp the enormity of his wild risk until the lenders tied up all his assets, nor did he realize his colossal mistake until he dug into the intricacies of the project. But it was too late. He was facing bankruptcy.

I met Larry on the street one day.

"George, I should've listened to you. I should've taken your deal."

All I could say was: "Larry, I'm sorry I wasn't persistent enough."

He worshiped a false god—bigness—and paid the price. He was sucked in by a false premise and lost his good sense and his life's savings.

HE FOLLOWED THE "BIGS," AND FELL INTO A TRAP

A Mr. Carr from a small town called me one day.

"I've read your books and solutions to some perplexing real estate problems. I've got one that perplexes me now. I've some excellent long-term assets but too many short-term debts. Do you have a few moments to listen to my problem?"

"Go ahead," I said.

A fifteen minute telephone conversation produced the following facts: He bought five tracts of land with small down payments, and custom built several homes and duplexes on each one. Then he got ambitious—he built 20 homes and duplexes on speculation, finishing them in 1974, the poorest real estate year in two decades. He over-leveraged in the worst of times. The balances on three of the sub-divisions became due and payable. His properties weren't selling or renting. And he couldn't meet the interest payments on his interim financing. He owed about $500,000 on his improved properties and $300,000 on his land.

"Will you level with me?" I asked, after I had a good hold on the sad statistics.

"Sure, go ahead."

"How much of your own money do you have in all these deals?"

"About $100,000."

"What do you think all your equities are worth?"

"About $250,000."

"What will you take?"

"I'd like to get my $100,000, but I'd settle for nothing if someone assumed my debts. The creditors are driving me crazy."

"I'll tell you what I'll do," I said. "I've made it a policy not to travel to see properties myself, but I know a subdivision expert who might bail you out."

Several days later my friend Charlie, the subdivision speculator, drove out to see Carr's properties. He spent an entire afternoon touring the town and appraising the subdivisions.

The next day, Charlie called me: "George, the man made too many mistakes. It got him into a trap from which only sudden good times could spring him loose. Instead of concentrating on one subdivision, he spread himself out on five, and instead of taking orders, he speculated in a market of limited absorptive capacity. And to compound his mistakes, the buildings have no style, quality, or attractive amenities. Your Mr. Carr tried to go big town in a small town and got burned. He's an awfully nice guy, but I see nothing there for me, and a lot less for him. I'm sorry."

I called Carr and gave him Charlie's report, ending with:

"But you're not looking for a lecture on overreaching. You want a solution."

"You're very kind," he said quietly.

"Let me offer a suggestion which worked in a case similar to yours. A man in Phoenix, Arizona did what you did—he overextended himself. He couldn't meet $1,800,000 in short-term debts against a $2,250,000 apartment project which the depression year, 1974, halted in its tracks. He needed another 18 months to make it a viable deal. The builder persuaded the interim lender not to foreclose but to pay him $20,000 a year to finish renting the apartments since he was more familiar with them than any man the bank could hire. The lender had no choice but to agree, since putting the man through bankruptcy and hiring another would diminish the bank's position still further.

"I suggest you go to your creditors," I continued, "and persuade them to hire you to pull them, and you, out of the hole. You've dug it, and you should know best how to get out. I guess that's all I can tell you."

"You've given me an idea I haven't thought about. I'd be willing to work for nothing if my creditors gave me time to clear up my debts and my name."

A year later I checked on Mr. Carr. Slowly he was getting his projects on their feet under the watchful eye of his banker.

"By 1976," he said, "I should be out of the woods, thanks to my understanding creditors."

Mr. Carr's case is symptomatic of the wild expansion malady which has plagued our country since the affluent 1960's. He caught the "bigness" virus from reading about the "bigs," and had he not fortunately been involved with patient creditors, he would have ended a bankrupt, as have thousands of others who relied on good times to make financial heroes out of them.

DON'T WALK TOO CLOSE TO THE PRECIPICE

Four is not better than one—if you're starting out in the hotel business. Paul found that out the hard way.

Several years ago, I was involved as a minor stockholder in Paul's company that successfully built apartments in many small Wisconsin towns. Then one day, Paul decided to build small motels in some of the towns. I suggested as a starter that he build one, and sell it to a mama-papa operator. He insisted on starting four at one time and operating them himself. I thought he was risking wildly. He thought they would turn out to be prudent investments. This hassle is described on pages 234 to 236 in *How Real Estate Fortunes Are Made*, if you care to follow the chronology of this interesting entrepreneurial effort.

Paul knew little about running hotels. After he built them, he turned the administration over to his secretary who knew less. She in turn hired managers who knew even less than she. To compound this chain of errors, Paul decided to go first class—in towns that were used to low rates. He spent $13,000 a room and geared his operations to $16 a night. What he didn't know was that a small-town motel guest is more interested in price than special amenities. He would have had a fighting chance to make a go of his four, 40-room motels had he spent $8,000 a room and charged $9 a night.

This miscalculation almost toppled his apartment-building empire. He invested almost all of its earnings in the four motels— $800,000 in cash in front of $1,200,000 in mortgages. He began losing money as soon as he opened. He lost $75,000 the first year, $25,000 the second year, barely broke even the third year, and now he is desperately trying to sell them. But who is going to pay him $800,000 to break even? The handwriting is on the wall—a wild risk can wipe out ten years of careful apartment-building profit.

Success comes from testing and growing. The old cliche, "Crawl before you walk," is sound advice when starting something new—especially the hotel business. But Faul began running before he learned to crawl, and so it's not surprising that he fell on his face.

He knew none of the secrets of building small hotels. He was so hypnotized by the "going first class" syndrome that instead of using wood shingles for the outside, which would have been adequate, he bought the most expensive brick. He installed elevators in two-story buildings. He spent $18,000 for art work in one motel's lobby. And he was "sold" the finest equipment for a full-service laundry in each of the four inns. All these amenities brought praise from those who stayed there, but there weren't enough of them to keep him in the black.

An austere mama-papa, 40-room operation could have easily made it in each of the four towns. By building for $8,000 a room and charging $9 a night, a middle-aged couple with a son or daughter to give a helping hand, and the incentive of ownership, could easily have made a good living in each of the motels.

However, I must soften my criticism somewhat because while I used Paul as an example of a wild risk, we must try to understand his reasoning. He had built apartment projects in some 35 different small towns of Wisconsin. They were all successful. In several towns, he was the first to introduce apartment living. He and his projects have been praised up and down the state. But there was such a great need for apartments in small towns that even where he made mistakes, they turned into successes. Perhaps because of this success, he thought he didn't have to be cautious in the motel market. He equated motels with apartments—a terrible mistake. Then to compound his mistake, he skipped the testing period—he violated the law of evolution by trying to grow too fast. He was trying to skip childhood which is neither natural nor prudent.

HE WAS TOO PERSUASIVE—HE MESMERIZED HIMSELF AND HIS LENDERS

This is the sad story of a rising young entrepreneur who was cut down by his own silver-tongued persuasiveness. When he was successful, lenders were putty in his hands, but when he couldn't deliver, he was putty in theirs—and they left him in a tragic mold. I knew Floyd when he was a millionaire, and now—a pauper.

He was a haberdasher who found the money-making pace too slow so he began dabbling in real estate. He did so well part time that he closed shop and turned his dabbling into full-time wheeling and dealing.

First, he built several dozen homes and sold them at a profit. Then he built several eight-families, using them as vehicles to sharpen his construction know-how and his ability to borrow money imaginatively. For instance, he never asked for a loan unless he brought along a complete set of plans and a beautiful colored rendering of the proposed project. This implanted a favorable picture in the lender's mind, which Floyd embellished with words to make it still more attractive.

For ten years, Floyd built and sold small apartments and office building projects—making money on each one. He was worth over a million dollars. But in 1966, with his cup running over, he caught the "bigitis" virus. Feverishly, he began accelerating his expansion plans—building more and bigger projects, and telescoping them into shorter periods of time. That was his undoing.

By 1968, he had $5,000,000 under construction—two apartment projects and three office buildings. In his hurry, he made the mistake of settling for secondary locations instead of waiting for the ideal ones. Then he made another serious miscalculation. Interest rates had begun to rise. Armed with his beautiful colored renderings and silver-tongued persuasiveness, he talked lending institutions into giving him temporary financing, with the hope of getting permanent mortgages at lower interest rates when the buildings were finished.

You guessed it! The interest rates went up, money became tighter and most serious of all, because he picked secondary locations, the projects weren't renting like his smaller, more sucessful ones. Then three things happened simultaneously—Floyd ran out of cash, out of brilliant talk, and out of time with the banks. They put on the squeeze; he squirmed and turned and pleaded, but to no avail. With $5,000,000 worth of buildings practically finished, and little rent coming in, the interest alone at $50,000 a month was enough to strangle him. After a year of agonizing travail, with debts and Floyd's blood pressure rising, the lenders made their moves. They foreclosed the five buildings, and because he had signed personally, they were able to take away all the assets Floyd had accumulated from his smaller, successful ventures. He could have weathered one or two projects—but not five.

But that wasn't all—the worst was yet to come. The emotional agitation of trying to keep five dying projects alive took its toll. As his empire began to collapse, he collapsed too—with a heart attack.

Several months after he got out of the hospital, he came to see me. He was looking for advice and a job. Gone was the cockiness of success. In its place, a flat, listless look—the mark of a physically and mentally defeated man.

"What would you like to do?" I asked.

"I don't know."

After we had talked about an hour, I asked:

"Any pearls of wisdom from one who's been at the top and the bottom?"

"It's funny, but you see a lot clearer from the bottom than from the top. When I was up there, I couldn't see the pitfalls below. My head was in the clouds. Now that I have slipped and fallen, I see more clearly. There was no need to expand so fast and gamble so foolishly. I let my ego ride me into bankruptcy—it's that simple and that dumb!" He trailed off sadly with a sigh and a shake of the head. The promising career of a wonderful guy was destroyed because he risked too wildly.

HOW A BIG GUN WAS REDUCED TO A POPGUN BECAUSE HE DIDN'T STUDY OUR CITY

A real estate tycoon who had successfully built large office buildings in several metropolitan areas in the South, decided to build one in our city. Initial successes can be blinding experiences, unless you're alert to changing conditions and false analogies.

Flushed with success and unaware that Milwaukee could be different from Memphis, Dallas or St. Louis, the conquering hero from below the Mason-Dixon Line began assembling land for a $4,000,000 office building in the wrong location, at the wrong time, and put the marketing of his office space in the wrong hands.

If a neophyte built a four-family making the same mistakes, it would be understandable, but for an experienced developer to plunge headlong into such a wild risk, was unbelievable.

I happened to have been negotiating for the same square block that he wanted for his office building and was quite familiar with it. I was trying to buy it for $500,000, and probably would have gotten it for that price, had he not rushed in and bought it for a million. That was his first mistake.

The Milwaukee River bisects the downtown, and traditionally, office space is more difficult to rent on the west side of the river than on the east side. He didn't know that—that was his second mistake. Also, Milwuakee's downtown office buildings were experiencing a 12 per cent vacancy, and higher west of the river. He didn't know that either, because when I met a young man at a Commercial Property Clinic in Chicago who happened to be in charge of leasing the office space for the new development, he was surprised to learn that the Milwaukee office-space market was weak, and that it was still weaker on the west side. He was a pleasant young man, but he didn't strike me as a ball of fire who could burn up a new town with impossible office space leasing records.

Nevertheless, on the strength of previous successes, the developer obtained a $3,000,000 temporary loan from a Southern bank and began construction. Apparently, the bank officials knew as little as he about the local conditions. The blind were leading the blind.

A year and a half later, the new twenty-story structure was 85 per cent completed and ten per cent rented—a ratio that's a prescription for failure. A year later, the tycoon developer gave up—he lost his rumored $300,000 equity money (he was sophisticated enough to limit his personal liability), he left $800,000 of unpaid contractors' bills, two years of delinquent real estate taxes and 18 months of interest arrearage on his $3,000,000 temporary bank loan. For a year, this wild risk fiasco bounced in and out of speculators' offices. Meanwhile, the city was waiting for its real estate taxes, the bank was worrying about collecting its interest and principal, and the contractors were fuming for their hard earned $800,000.

Fortunately, for all concerned, an astute young man stepped into the picture and with a few deft, unorthodox moves, obtained title to the collapsing deal. Without a dime of his own money, he put it on its feet by leasing 50 per cent of its space and then finding an angel who bought the building's losses with his hundreds of thousands of dollars of ordinary income. This "angel" was indeed angelic. Instead of wiping out the contractors, as he could have done, he paid them 90 cents on the dollar and saved several from bankruptcy.

Ten years later, the building is a going concern (thanks to a millionaire coming to its rescue), but nevertheless, from the developmental standpoint, it was a colossal flop—an example of one who risked wildly—and lost.

5

There's a Bigger Income in Small Real Estate Enterprises Than in Big Ones

The economic philosophy behind this concept is profoundly important. It makes the point that there's higher productivity per person in a small, personalized business than in an impersonalized, large one. And what's more important, the by-product of this economic law builds a stronger democracy. Let me illustrate.

ONE BUILDING 100% OCCUPIED
CAN MAKE MORE MONEY
THAN TEN BUILDINGS 80% OCCUPIED

Chuck, a friend of mine, owns a 50,000 square foot office building that's been fully occupied for years. His income is $250,000 a year, and the fixed expenses $125,000, leaving a net income before debt service of $125,000. Because Chuck owns only one building, he's able to give it his undivided attention—that's why his fixed expenses are only 50 per cent of his gross rent.

Another friend of mine, Leonard, owns ten buildings comprising 500,000 square feet which, at 100 per cent occupancy at $5 a square foot, would bring $2,500,000 in annual rent. But because he's involved in several other businesses besides owning these buildings, he can't give them his personal attention. And because of it, they are only 90 per cent occupied, and his rent is 90 per cent of a potential $2,500,000, or $2,250,000. His fixed expenses on the ten buildings are high—60 per cent of the potential gross rent, or $1,500,000.

Let's assume Chuck's mortgage is $750,000 payable in 25 years at 8 per cent, and let's further assume that Leonard's debt, amortization and interest are proportionate to Chuck's. Therefore, Leonard's mortgages would be 10 times $750,000 or $7,500,000 amortized in 25 years at 8 per cent.

Here's the clinching argument. Leonard, with ten buildings, has a $50,000 cash flow, while Chuck, with one building, has a $55,000 cash flow. The table below shows it graphically.

CHUCK'S 50,000 SQUARE FOOT BUILDING

		Debt Service on	
100% Occupied	50% Fixed Expenses	$750,000	Cash Flow
$250,000 rent	$125,000	$70,000	$55,000

LEONARD'S TEN BUILDINGS COMPRISING 500,000 SQUARE FEET

		Debt Service on	
90% Occupied	60% Fixed Expenses	$7,500,000	Cash Flow
$2,250,000 rent	$1,500,000	$700,000	$50,000

HERE'S WHAT HAPPENS WHEN LEONARD'S TEN BUILDINGS ARE 85% OCCUPIED

		Debt Service on	
85% Occupied	60% Fixed Expenses	$7,500,000	Cash Flow (Minus)
$2,125,000 rent	$1,500,000	$700,000	($75,000)

This analysis pinpoints the extremely important economic fact that dollar for dollar, personalized property ownership and management is far more profitable than hastily amassed property that's impersonally managed.

But there's a more important factor than economics involved here. Let me underscore it with a discussion between Karl Menninger, of the famed psychiatric Menninger Clinic, and a doctor of economics, which I heard when I attended a seminar at the Aspen Institute of Humanistic Studies in Colorado.

"The small farmer, corner grocery man, and corner druggist," Dr. Menninger said, "were far happier in their small-scale enterprises than today's farm hands in the huge combines or clerks in national food and drug chains."

"But you couldn't have low prices without mass production," the economic expert countered.

"From our extensive research," Dr. Menninger replied, "we can tell you what gives people stability and happiness. I would think it's more important to bend economics to people than people to economics. Do you want a nation of well-fed, other-directed automatons, or spontaneous, self-directed people with incentives to be creative?"

I can't speak authoritatively outside my field, but in real estate, I couldn't agree with Dr. Menninger more. I've seen the dead hand of lethargy, disloyalty, and larceny among those who work for large realty companies; and the joyful bounce of the owner-manager who instills the same personalized enthusiasm in his small circle of associates.

As the "bigs" grow weaker and the "smalls" grow stronger, we'll come back to the human scale. We'll rebel against seeing people as dots from tall buildings. That's for the birds, not humans. We'll decentralize more and computerize less. We're going to "bend economics to people," because when our psyches become alienated enough, like the prodigal son, we'll come back to the more personalized human scale. It's the ideal milieu in which a democracy can flourish.

WHY A BUILDING EARNED LESS AND LESS AS IT GOT INTO BIGGER AND BIGGER HANDS

Let me zero in specifically on what can happen when an owner-managed building is sold to a multi-million dollar public realty company.

In 1965, I sold the 200,000 square foot Bockl Building to a New York based $100,000,000 public realty company. The building then showed a cash flow of $160,000 a year after fixed expenses and debt service on a $2,800,000 first mortgage. The public company paid me $1,000,000 in cash and a $600,000 second mortgage, a price tailored to a 13 per cent cash flow return on its $1,000,000 investment—a good deal, especially when it also included about $50,000-a-year amortization on the first and second mortgages.

But its remote management soon began to change the tenants' attitudes and the building's environment. Rent checks were now sent to a strange company in New York, instead of to George Bockl, whom the tenants knew personally. New tenants were not receiving flowers when they moved in, and the maintenance man stopped making his rounds to ask if there was anything that needed repairing.

My manager, whom the new owners retained, now had to make on-the-spot policy decisions as daily crises arose. He was a good man with my guidance, but only fair without it. Left alone, he would debate with tenants to win points, not realizing that the more he won, the greater were the chances of losing them as tenants. And the $12,000-a-year manager was no match when it came to negotiating leases with shrewd executives who were experts at cutting expenses. Occasionally the national or regional manager would fly in for a day or two to look in on a maintenance or lease problem, but pressed for time, he was only able to feather touch the situation. His effectiveness was weakened because the tenant felt the rush, and either took advantage of it, or backed away and began thinking about moving elsewhere.

Five years after I sold the Bockl Building, I heard through the grapevine that the $160,000 yearly cash flow dropped to $75,000, and that the new owners were trying to sell.

Within a year, the building was sold to an $800,000,000 Miami based real estate conglomerate for $4,000,000. They fired the local manager and put in one of their own. They then replaced him with a succession of new managers while the fixed expenses kept going up and the occupancy, down.

In 1975, I offered to sell to the Miami owners my $500,000 second mortgage balance for $375,000 cash. They refused, and instead asked me to buy the Bockl Building. Before inquiring into the price, I asked the key question:

"What's the cash flow after fixed expenses and debt service?"

"$30,000 negative cash flow," was the answer over the 'phone from 2,500 miles away. "But," the voice urged persuasively, "there're about $200,000 a year of vacancies that could turn this building around into a great money maker."

Then I asked the price.

"$4,000,000," came the unabashed reply.

Well, this building will obviously not sell for $4,000,000. When this huge realty company has mismanaged it enough with its remote control, it'll get tired of losses, and a small operator will buy it for perhaps $3,250,000, and make a huge success of it.

Let's not be awed by the expertise of the big operators. While I agree that they're wizards with figures, corporate structure, and modern administrative methods, they are woefully weak where it counts most—getting personalized management to deliver high-return cash-flow income.

And no wonder! A landlord-tenant relationship, by its very nature, should be a personal one, a sort of host-guest relationship. When it's diluted with impersonal red tape, as it is in a big realty company, it tends to become more socialistic and less capitalistic. By that I mean that bureaucracy takes over, and what's bureaucracy but another name for bigness. Since there's very little difference between socialistic and capitalistic bureaucracy, the commercial barons who tout capitalism out of one side of their mouths and conglomerate out of the other—are incongruous. They weaken capitalism for socialistic take over.

The way to a stable and viable capitalism is, as Menninger suggests, opting for an economic climate where small businesses can flourish. That's when we'll have happier people and greater productivity.

The wise real estate man will stop following the Pied Piper of bigness and begin appreciating the profit potential of smallness.

Let a hundred small enterprises joyfully bloom
Where a giant once cast his shadow of impersonalized gloom.

BIGNESS NOT ONLY PRODUCES IMPERSONALIZATION BUT OFTEN ENDS IN A BIG BUST

A former classmate of mine headed up a small $5,000,000 real estate trust. The stock came out at ten and hovered a point or two above for several years. It never paid less than 8 per cent to its shareholders. I was familiar with its investment portfolio—it was small but sound.

Then in the late 1960's, my friend was hit with the "expansionitis virus," and on the strength of his success with his small real estate trust, he sold another $45,000,000 of stock, and quickly invested it in projects throughout the country.

Within two years, everything began to change—my friend, the investment portfolio, the rate of return and the value of the stock. My friend's face took on a harried look, the properties were rife with vacancies, the rate of return plummeted to zero and the stock dropped to $3 a share. The reasons were threefold—the economy took a downward turn, properties were bought too quickly, and management lost the former personal touch.

Had the real estate trust stayed at $5,000,000, it could have weathered the financial turbulence by tightening its expenses and holding on. But with $50,000,000 worth of property quickly amassed and impersonally managed, the problems grew to unmanageable proportions. The expanded capital brought contracted returns. Dollar for dollar, the smaller real estate trust brought ten times the cash flow the larger one did.

A CRASH THAT RESOUNDED IN A DOZEN BANKS

Fifteen years ago, I sold a 20-acre wooded parcel to a young man who put it to its highest and best use—a 200-apartment project that was extremely successful. I knew he did it on a shoestring because it took two years before I got my $90,000 for the land. Every time he asked for an extention of his debt, he did it in a forthright, gentlemanly manner. I had a feeling this young man was going to go far. He went too far.

In 15 years, he built thousands of apartments into a $400,000,000 empire. He was a fine, friendly young man when he started, and because I haven't seen him since, I don't know what kind of a man he is today. But I do know something about the alienation that infected his far-flung organization.

I interviewed a young man for a managerial job who worked in his national holding firm.

"Did you leave or were you fired," I asked when he identified the company.

"I left."

"Why?"

"I couldn't stomach the confusion, disloyalty, and graft that went on. I have a religious orientation, and I could see that if I didn't bend, they'd break me. Yours is a small organization, I think I could be happy working for you."

In 1974, this top-of-the-heap building complex collapsed, and its creditors pounced on it.

This is an excellent example of how remote control alienates those below into a corruption that bloats building costs, swells managerial expenses, and accelerates vacancies. All that's needed to tilt such a highly leveraged, quickly built, and impersonalized empire, is for the economy to slide just a little—perhaps a 10 per cent rise in vacancies—and it can start tumbling down.

This one did, with a crash that reverberated in the quiet back offices of a dozen banks.

YOU CAN SEE BETTER CLOSE-UP
THAN FROM 1,200 MILES AWAY

After I sold my Bockl Building, I flew to New York to meet the administrative team that was behind the $100,000,000 public realty company. Since they still owed me $600,000, I wanted to meet the men who wielded the power.

The president was a crisp, capable fellow who, with a great deal of pride, showed me his elaborate accounting system by which he charted how each property in their national investment portfolio was doing. Then I met the heads of the hotel, office building, shopping center, and apartment divisions. They were bright, administratively oriented executives, but I'm sure the head of the office building division didn't know one tenth what I knew about my city and about the Bockl Building. Yet, the economic fate of the $4,100,000 Bockl Building depended on him and on the on-site manager who needed daily guidance that wasn't there.

With the superficial knowledge the division manager had of the some 20 office buildings spread from New York to California, all he could do was feather touch them with his infrequent visits and hope that the local manager could carry out what little knowledge he could pass on to him. And I suppose that's what happened in each of the other divisions.

The cumulative effect of this kind of remote control management took its toll, not only on the Bockl Building but on their entire investment portfolio. In a few years, the various buildings which the public company bought from individual owners began to lose their cash flows, and the stock dropped from $16 to $2 a share. All the modern administrative techniques couldn't match the more basic ingredient of on the spot, owner-manager attention.

The president and his divisional managers have long since left the company. Its real estate has been sold, its name changed and it is now engaged in another business. The New York executives weren't able to generate the profit from the properties like the small owners who sold it to them. The public company officials weren't able to buy incentive, pride of ownership, and the profits that go with them.

LIKE THE DINOSAUR,
THIS COMPANY GOT TOO BIG TO SURVIVE

Here is a clinching argument that should make us lose our awe for the "bigs."

A bright young man who helped me lease space in the Bockl Building, decided he was ready for bigger game on the East Coast, and landed a job with the largest realty firm in New York. I kept in touch with him. One day he came to Milwaukee to visit me.

"The in-fighting, elbowing, and selfish aggressiveness of the executives in the organization jarred me," he said, "and I was no timid lilly, you'll remember." Indeed he was not.

"What exactly shook you?" I asked.

"Everyone's for himself. There's no loyalty. Everyone is in a hurry. There's no time or inclination to develop a personal relationship like you and I had. And there's a lot of waste."

After several years, he left the well-known, giant company and went into business for himself. He was not suave enough, thick skinned enough, or expeditious enough to keep up with the big boys.

The president and the running mates of that company ran too fast and in too many directions. The result—they lost touch with each other. The nitty-gritty was neglected and dry rot set in. The fixed expenses of the multi-million dollar real estate empire went up, the occupancy down. In spite of all their expertise, they couldn't save their company. It nose-dived into bankruptcy. The real estate giant of New York, like the dinosaur, was no more. It got too big to survive. Let's not have this lesson wasted on us.

HOW A SMALL SUBURB FELL PREY TO BIGNESS

The idea that bigness is progress has also invaded the suburbs—often with sad and ludicrous results. Here's what happened to a village of 20,000.

The mayor wanted to show his constituents that he could think big, and to impress them, he hired a real estate expert to make a feasibility study for building a 100-room hotel, a 75,000 square foot office building, three large apartment projects, and a 1,000-car underground parking garage covered with a beautifully landscaped mall on four acres of land. A grandiose scheme, and economically impractical. The real estate counselor must have been taken in by the mayor's euphoria, because alas, he found the plan feasible.

The grand idea got off to a faltering start with a 100-unit highrise and then sputtered to a halt. The rest of the plan couldn't be financed because it called for another $10,000,000 in improvements in an area that couldn't support more than $2,000,000.

But what the mayor lacked in knowledge, he made up in frothy aggressiveness. Using eminent domain and bulldozer persuasion, he had the village acquire the homes and small stores on the four-acre site, razed them and kept inviting investors to build. The knowledgeable developers didn't move beyond the mayor's inspirational pitch, but the unknowledgeable ones spent tens of thousands of dollars on preliminary plans, only to be turned down by lenders.

The mayor, the expert and prospective builders didn't fully understand the hazards of overimprovement. It was an excellent site for a carefully planned, $4,000,000 development, but not for a wild $12,000,000 spending spree. After 15 years of huffing and puffing, the sad site of weeds and razed buildings is still there—mute testimony that bigness doesn't pay.

LEWIS MUMFORD AND ROBERT ARDREY OFFER SANE URBAN ADVICE

Undaunted by failure of the mall due to planned overimprovement, the mayor and his unpaid trustees stumbled onto another blunder. They bought ten acres for $1,000,000 from a public utility and offered the tract to developers for building apartment projects.

They visualized five high-rise buildings, comprising about 1,000 units. Again their bigness virus acted up and blinded their vision.

The village fathers made several mistakes. First, they overpaid for the land. Second, they compounded it by justifying the purchase price on the basis of rezoning the site for 1,000 apartments in order to lower the per unit cost of the land. But their major premise was wrong. The surrounding area was already congested, and to add another 1,000 units was not only wrong, in human terms, but economically indigestible. After all, this was not the Chicago Loop.

After eight years, only one high-rise building of 120 apartments has been built on the site. The rest of the land is growing weeds. Had the city planners been satisfied with 200 garden apartments for the entire ten acres, it could have been a pleasant oasis in the midst of helter-skelter congestion. Had the mayor and his trustees read Lewis Mumford's books on sane urbanization, they would have realized that 20 families to the acre is the optimum for human-scale living. And had they read Robert Ardrey's, *The Social Contract,* they would have been shocked at their callous disregard in squeezing 1,000 families on ten acres. Ardrey, biologist and anthropologist, has been exploding a series of philosophical landmines. He has shown experimentally that rats are docile when they have lots of room; they become ferocious when their living space is narrowed, and cannibalistic when they're confined in a congested area. This lesson should not be wasted on humans.

THE THEORY THAT BIGNESS IS PROGRESS DIES HARD

You would think the village elders would learn. But they didn't —the bigness virus had debilitated their thinking.

After two sad failures, the village mayor and his cohorts, rezoned a 20-acre bluff overlooking Lake Michigan for 285 condominiums. It sloped 50 feet to the water on the east, and to the west high on the bluff, the land was fringed by eight old but charming mansions. It was in the heart of an area of luxurious homes.

A developer, entranced by the superb location and the liberal, come-on zoning, optioned the land and the eight landmark homes for $1,000,000. He spent $50,000 for elaborate plans preparatory to building the $15,000,000 lake-terrace condominiums.

But this time, the residents acted. They formed a residential association to block this ill-conceived development. Since I was a resident of the suburb and a member of the association, I was invited to a meeting of the developers, the citizen opponents and the village officials. Its purpose was to find a way out of the impasse.

"The developers ought to thank their opposition for blocking their plans," I said during the discussion. "The project has all the earmarks for economic failure."

"Why?" one of the developers shot at me sharply.

"Because razing those eight mansions would shoot your land cost sky high—and needlessly."

"What do you suggest?"

"Leave the homes where they are and build down below. This will accomplish two things—one good for you, and the other good for the village. First, for you: It'll reduce the cost of your land because you can resell the homes for about $650,000, so the remaining 15 acres will cost you only $350,000. And for the village: The bluff area with its eight magnificent homes will remain untouched, and since the project will be down by the water where it won't be seen from the street it will be more exclusive."

"But that'll cut down the number of condominiums," the developer argued.

"That's exactly what we want, and it's to your advantage," I replied. "Fifty luxury condominiums hidden among the trees and overlooking the water will sell easily, while a big project like 285 condominiums on top of the bluff and down the slope, could give you a big financial headache. And besides, there's something else to think about—we, the people. Can't you see—we don't want to change the character of the village—the homes on the bluff overlooking the lake are part of its character." Turning to the village officials, I said, "Fifty units may give you a smaller tax base, but it'll blend better with the character of the village."

I then spent a few minutes philosophizing on Lewis Mumford's and Robert Ardrey's insights. This was new thinking for the village officials and the developers, and they listened with rapt attention. I don't know whether Mumford and Ardrey had anything to do with it, but a few months later the developer withdrew his 285 unit project and changed it to the 50 luxury condominium concept. That's where it stands today.

I don't want to leave the impression that the mayor and his trustees are not capable and well-meaning men. They are, but like millions of others, they've been subliminally conditioned by bigness and are unwittingly playing out their conditioned roles. Had any of them read *Small Is Beautiful,* by E.F. Schumacher, dealing with the ecological imperativeness of returning to small-scale enterprise in order to prevail on our planet earth, they wouldn't have fallen prey to the "bigitis" virus.

HOW I WAS ALMOST PURSUADED TO GO PUBLIC

The story of the Pied Piper is an allegory for children, but often mature men are siren-songed too. It almost happened to me 12 years ago. My piper was a nationally known Realtor and the song he played was profit.

He was as persuasive as he was astute. He was worth about $30,000,000, and he saw a chance to make another one or two million by combining a few scattered pieces of real estate he owned in New York and Chicago with mine and going public. It was a logical deal for him because his scraps of real estate—vacant land—would appraise for a couple of million (in his estimation), and added to my income property, they would form a good nucleus for a public company.

"First we get good appraisals for your property and my land," he said. "Then we sell 50 per cent of it to the public for cash, which we can keep. Next we float new issues of either stocks or bonds, buy more real estate, and away we go."

What swayed me was that he had an excellent reputation and frankly, I was flattered that he was interested in me. Or was it my good income properties? He probably forgot all about me after the meeting, busy as he was with his national wheeling and dealing, but I squirmed in indecision for weeks before I made up my mind not to go public.

The question of amassing wealth at the cost of it being my single concern, was already bubbling in my mind. I had met many prominent wheeler-dealers who had churned themselves into calculating machines, and I didn't like what I saw. The following incident helped crystalize my thinking.

A real estate tycoon came to town to negotiate a deal with me. He was all business—no warmth. I could see he was more interested in numbers than people. The shocker came when he said, "You know, it's tougher to get a decent call girl in your town than in any I've visited."

"Are you married?" I asked. My question must have sounded accusatory because he reacted sharply with, "Yeh, and I love my wife. But what's that got to do with call girls?"

"It's got this to do with it. If you break a contract with someone you love, aren't you just as apt to break it with a stranger?" His cheeks crimsoned.

"Then I advise you to keep your hands in your pockets," he snapped

"I will." Our deal fell apart.

If aggressive growth is not tamed by a counter desire for quality living, it can easily degenerate into the foolish game of growth just for the hell of it.

Had I gone public, I would have been hurrying from property to property across the country, analyzing apartments, office buildings, and shopping center projects. I would have had to dilute the loyal and personal relationships I had built in my city for less loyal and impersonal ones. And probably, I would have ended up the way many big moguls did—on the brink of bankruptcy.

My economic instincts sounded the alarm against going national. But that was only the below-surface reason. My main concern was that by going public I would lose the personal and private relationship I had built up with my family. I would be tempted to give priority to success over spending more time at home. I know that many sophisticated colleagues will raise an eyebrow at this, and smile it away as a lot of sentimental nonsense, but I've seen enough harried faces with desire-laden minds to know that they're wrong and I'm right. It's almost impossible to bridge the gap that develops when ambitious growth is given priority over family interests. Only the extremely wise can walk that tightrope. Most of us have to pay the high price of family alienation for playing the growth game. It's not worth it!

HOW SMALL-SCALE INVESTORS SUCCESSFULLY BUILT YEARLY RETIREMENT INCOMES

I know how these men got started and I know how they finished. While you don't necessarily have to emulate them, still, their experiences should give you some insights in fashioning your own investment careers.

An Unsuccessful Attorney Becomes a Successful Investor

Jerry became a lawyer not out of an intense desire to practice law, but to get a general education. He stumbled unsuccessfully in his profession for several years and then, at the suggestion of a friend, bought a four-family. He liked dealing with his tenants more than he did with his clients. There was less pressure and more profit. He bought another four-family. As his interest in the practice of law waned, his interest in real estate waxed. In a few years he closed his law practice and opened a small real estate management firm.

Now, 20 years later, at 48, he owns 300 rental units grossing about $400,000 a year. My guess is that he enjoys a cash flow of about $40,000 a year, and in 20 years he will be independently wealthy. He probably could never have done it in law. I play golf with him occasionally, and because he enjoys a pressureless life, his golf score is 10 strokes less than mine. Another reason is that he's a better driver, chipper, and putter than I am. With his specialized apartment investing know-how, he built a prosperous, leisurely life style. You can do it, too.

An Engineer Converts His Knowledge into Building Small but Successful Commercial Projects

Wayne made a good living as a civil engineer for a large manufacturing company. A friend of his asked for his help in designing a duplex for resale. When Wayne showed him some money saving short-cuts, resulting in his friend's earning several thousand dollars, he began looking for a similar deal for himself.

He didn't have to wait long. His friend reciprocated the favor by giving him the name of a company that wanted to lease a fast-food restaurant. Wayne called its representative, and after some negotiations he built a small restaurant for $150,000, including land, and leased it to the food chain for 20 years at $12,000 net per year. That was 20 years ago when interest was 5 per cent. He mortgaged out and had about $1,500 left after payments on his $150,000 loan.

He negotiated and built the small restaurant in his spare time. After making several similar deals, he quit his job and devoted his full time to building an investment portfolio. His forte was in building at less than prevailing costs by buying and warehousing odd lot building materials, such as lumber, cement blocks, electric fixtures, plumbing fixtures, etc. When he combined this material saving with the labor saving resulting from hiring small low-overhead contractors, he invariably was able to finance his small buildings at 100 per cent.

With about a $100,000-a-year cash flow, he's now enjoying a leisurely, aristocratic life, traveling to the far corners of the world while his tenants are paying off his $2,000,000 mortgages. And it all started when he was asked to help out a friend. I guess you can say, when you give, you get.

A Hebrew Teacher Relieves His Poverty by Investing in Real Estate

There's no way for a Hebrew teacher to do better than eke out a meager living. That's because there are few children scrambling to learn Hebrew. Abraham enjoyed teaching, but he didn't like the low pay. With his more than average intelligence he began looking for an answer. The father of one of his pupils bragged how easy it was to make money in real estate. Abraham listened. "How?"

"Get some wealthy fellow to loan you several thousand dollars, and buy an income property," he urged Abraham. "That'll give you the extra income you're looking for."

"How about you being the angel?" Abraham asked. He caught the parent by surprise.

"Well...," he hesitated, "I may."

That was enough for Abraham. He found a four-family and asked his friend to back him. He did.

Abraham discovered that he was as good a property manager as he was a teacher. He managed to get a few other backers and away he went. He bought more and more property, and with the inflationary wind at his back, he soon paid off his old backers and found new ones. Within 10 years his life style changed completely. With $20,000 a year cash flow he now taught Hebrew as a hobby not as a necessity.

"George," he told me about 15 years ago when he was at the height of his success, "I'm amazed that so few people know how easy it is to make money in real estate."

He is right.

A Dancing Master Glides into a Small Real Estate Fortune

A lithe-looking man came to my office one day and said, "I'd like to buy your Knickerbocker Hotel."

He took me by surprise. I collected myself and began to question him. Here was his story.

He loved to dance and made his living teaching it, but there was little money in it. He borrowed several thousand dollars from his father and started buying rooming houses. He did so well that in a few years, he had accumulated enough equities to trade them in for a 40-family. Inflation soon blew up his equity in the apartment building to $150,000.

"Now," he said to me, "I'm ready to trade it for your $2,000,000 Knickerbocker Hotel."

"Wait a minute," I said. "I think you're flying too high. You've done very well so far, but now you're taking too big a jump. You don't have enough equity, nor may I add, enough experience to handle a big hotel."

I discouraged him and nothing came of it. But he made me think as he sauntered lithely out of my office. If a dancing master who, in my estimation, didn't have too much savvy, could make it in investment real estate, then whoever you are reading this, take courage and give it a try. You may be pleasantly surprised.

From Peddling Watermelons to Traveling the Length and Breadth of the Earth

Peter had a yen for traveling to far away places, but he knew he could never realize his dreams by buying and selling watermelons. He didn't have much of an education, but he was loaded with common sense.

With the little money he earned huckstering watermelons, he bought rundown core properties, fixed them up and carefully selected tenants who would maintain them. He quickly earned the reputation as the core landlord with the cleanest and best-maintained flats. He capitalized on this reputation to get loans on neglected properties where less qualified managers couldn't.

For five years, he continued to sell watermelons while building his investment portfolio in cheap properties. Then his side-line became his main line. He quit selling watermelons and put his buying, fixing, and renting of old properties in high gear. Within 10 years, he was drawing rent from about 150 units and earning about $35,000 a year.

Now that he had the money to realize his life's dream, he did it up brown. He quit working and started traveling—two months down the Amazon on a raft in Brazil, another three months in Nepal, every year a new country for months at a time. His wife took care of the properties while he was away on his rugged, adventurous jaunts. He's 60 now, and taking it easy except when he's getting in shape for some arduous journey. When I saw him last year I asked, "Where now?"

"Mongolia," he replied with a smile.

"For how long?"

"About three months."

That's what investment real estate did for him. What would you like it to do for you?

Men Who Dabbled in Investment Real Estate and Made More Money Dabbling than in Their Professions

Economics Professor

George's $15,000-a-year teaching salary provided him with a living wage, but the 70 rental units he had somehow acquired during the last 10 years added something extra. They gave him $15,000-a-year cash flow while he was teaching, but more importantly, he'll retire in grand style 20 years from now.

There are not many professors doing it, but more ought to. It's far less complicated than teaching economics.

Physician

Dr. M.W. is one of the leading surgeons in our city. At 40, he was already netting about $100,000 a year before income taxes. That's when he started investing in real estate.

Now at 55, he's still earning about $125,000 from his medical practice, but in addition, he's payed off several hundred thousand dollars on his properties during the last 15 years. Inflation has added another $200,000 to his equities, so that now he's worth about $500,000. At 65, his medical income will no doubt taper off, but by then, his apartment investments will be free and clear and worth about $1,000,000. His yearly income from his real estate should be about $100,000 to $125,000 a year, or about the same as when his medical income was at its height.

How did he do all this? He would simply O.K. the purchase of the properties and his wife would follow through with their management. Thus his mind wasn't preoccupied with the business detail that might interfere with his exacting work, but was only as a pleasant conversational piece when he and his wife relaxed over a cup of coffee.

It was easy, pleasant, and profitable. I recommend this kind of real estate investment for every high-earning physician in the land. It makes a lot of sense—and dollars too.

Attorney

A.W. practiced law until he was 65. He wasn't a great lawyer, but he was a good lawyer. His average yearly earnings were about $25,000 for 40 years. There was no way he could have retired in grand style on this income while raising a family and paying taxes. But because he managed to get into apartment deals with partners, with backers, and by himself, beginning way back in the thirties, he was able to acquire enough income properties to sell out for a million dollars in cash upon his retirement.

With some $700,000 stashed away in treasury bills (the safest investment there is) he's now spending six months in Florida, three months in his home town and three months traveling the far corners of the globe.

During his 40 years of dabbling in real estate while he was working hard as a lawyer, he earned as much in his avocation as he did in his vocation. If you seriously study the various approaches to building a yearly income described in this book, there's no reason why you shouldn't enjoy your retirement the way this attorney is doing. Don't let your future unravel aimlessly, begin planning it 40 years in advance

Businessman

A.S. is the most successful formal-attire renter in our city. He covers our metropolitan area with five stores. He's a busy man, but not too busy to build stores on speculation and finding the tenants to fill them.

Here's how he does it. Being a storekeeper himself, he has a nose for good locations. When he finds one, he warehouses it until he gets a tenant who likes his site. But instead of building one store, he builds three and invariably, the other two are leased within a year.

He's now drawing rent from some 15 stores in six locations.

"It's fun," he tells me when we talk about his real estate at Rotary meetings. "It's so easy and profitable, and it gets my mind off my business."

About 15 years from now, when he quits his formal-wear leasing business, I wouldn't be surprised if his earnings from the sale of his real estate will not equal the total earnings from his business. You see, what you earn in business or as a salary increases arithmetically, but what you earn in investment real estate increases geometrically—in three ways—cash flow, amortization, and inflation.

It's these multi-dimensional factors plus good management that enables small investors like the professor, doctor, lawyer, and businessman to multiply their investment ten-fold when it is planned early and selectively chosen. You don't need to get into big deals to make big money. The little ones often do better than the big ones. This is not pie in the sky. You've just read the actual cases where men like you have done it. I share this with you in the hope you will be encouraged to do likewise.

6

Answers to Readers' Questions That Made a Lot of Money for Them

Sharing knowledge is the life blood of the civilizing process. Sharing enriches the giver and the receiver.

In the ensuing pages, readers of my books present real estate problems which taxed my ingenuity. In trying to solve them, I had to dig deep into my reservoir of experience and come up with insights, which if not for the questions, would never have surfaced. So you see, I'm as grateful for the questions which honed my knowledge, as I hope my readers were helped, when they got my answers.

That's sharing—a two-way learning encounter that humanizes relationships and produces benefits.

A TELEPHONE TIP CONVERTS $9,000 TO A $35,000-A-YEAR ANNUITY

An attorney from a small town near Pittsburgh who read my book, *How Real Estate Fortunes Are Made,* called one day, and asked for a solution to this problem:

"I own a building with a single tenant—a bank. Its $25,000-a-year lease is expiring and the bank wants to buy my property for

$250,000 and spend another $500,000 to modernize it. I've depreciated my building to zero, and if I sell it, I won't have much more than $150,000 after taxes. If I invest it in a savings-and-loan at say 6 per cent, my income'll shrink to $9,000 a year. Got some idea how I can do better than that?"

I gave it a few moments thought, and then an idea struck me.

"Tell the bank president," I said, slowly gathering my thoughts, "that you'll spend $500,000 to upgrade your building and lease it to him for 30 years."

"But I don't have the money."

"Borrow it."

"From whom?"

"From the bank—your present lessee. Get a $500,000 mortgage at 7 per cent, the current interest rate on a 30-year amortization, so the loan terminates at the same time as the bank's 30-year lease. Then net lease the remodeled building to the bank based on a value of $750,000, with a return rate of 10 per cent, or $75,000 a year. Now listen carefully. Since your payments on the $500,000, 30-year mortgage will be about $40,000 a year, you'll be left with a cash flow of $35,000 a year. That's a lot better than selling it and being left with $9,000 a year.

"And there's another advantage," I continued. "Your $35,000 will be partially tax sheltered, especially during the first ten years, when depreciation will be at its maximum. When you compare this $35,000 tax sheltered income to your $9,000 ordinary income, the advantages should become obvious."

"I'm beginning to get what you're driving at," the attorney said, "and I want to thank you for a wonderful suggestion. But I can see the bank president saying to me, 'You want to borrow $500,000 at 7 per cent, yet you want $75,000 rent based on a 10 per cent return.' How do I counter that?"

I thought for a while and tried this idea for a starter.

"How old are you?" I asked.

"Fifty-five."

"You'll be 85 when this $35,000 annuity ends. Why don't you sweeten the deal by agreeing to convey the property to the bank for one dollar at the end of 30 years, or for some nominal sum like $25,000. Or some larger sum that is mutually agreeable, and will compensate them for the extra 3 per cent."

"That's not a bad idea either, because I won't be needing much at 85—if I live that long."

"Your heirs may not like this plan, but my concern is to get you the most spendable money during your lifetime. This, in my estimation, does it. You can refine it, but don't change the guts of the plan. The more I think of it, the better I like it."

"You've given me lots to think about and I'm grateful. Any charge for this?"

"No," I said, "your payment is having presented me with an interesting item for my next book. You see, I benefit you and hopefully, your problem will benefit others."

"Well, thanks again." And he hung up.

A half-year later, I received a letter outlining a plan which the attorney prepared for the bank, similar to the one I suggested. He indicated there was a good chance for its adoption.

TRADING PROPERTIES CAN BE HAZARDOUS IF YOU DON'T UNDERSTAND THE DANGERS

Several years ago, I received a call from a Chicago schoolteacher.

"I've read your books, and I like your solutions to the many interesting real estate problems. I have one that's got me on the fence. Mind giving me some advice?"

"What's your problem?"

"I own several duplexes with small mortgages. The income is about $15,000, and I clear about $7,000 a year. In your book, *How Real Estate Fortunes Are Made,* you devote several pages to trading up. The idea fascinates me, but I'm a little afraid."

"What are you afraid of?"

"Well, a real estate broker has suggested a trade deal which he explained as follows: The owner of a 120-apartment building is willing to take my four duplexes in trade as a down payment on his apartment complex, if I assume a million dollar first mortgage and a $400,000 second. The deal tempts me, but I'm afraid of those huge debts, even though the income is there to cover them."

"You should be scared. You're taking a big jump. You'll recall that in my book I use the example of trading up from an 8-family to a 20, then perhaps to a 40. But in each case, I suggest you consolidate your position before taking the next step. You're taking too many steps in this exchange. But let's dig a little deeper. First, what's the gross income from the 120 apartments? And can you tell me the amount of the cash flow after all fixed expenses and debt service on the first and second mortgages?"

"The gross rental is $220,000 a year, and the fixed expenses plus payments on both mortgages is $200,000, or a cash flow of $20,000 compared to my present cash flow of $7,000. That's why I'm interested."

"Please look at your statement. Is the $220,000 gross rental based on 100 per cent occupancy?"

"Yes it is, and it's 100 per cent occupied."

"To play it safe, you should reconstruct the rental on the basis of 95 per cent occupancy. That would give you a realistic gross of about $209,000. Now check your statement again. How much do they allow for painting?"

"I don't see anything for painting."

"H'm.... Provision for the vacancy factor and painting has already more than wiped out your $20,000 cash flow."

"But they're allowing me $150,000 for my equity in the duplexes, and between you and me, they only cost me $50,000."

"But between you and me, they probably have $250,000 of water in the deal. Do you know what I mean by that?"

"I guess so. It's $250,000 overpriced so they can be generous and allow $150,000 on my duplexes."

"You're getting the picture. This is not a good deal for you. A 5 per cent rise in operating costs could wipe you out. It's too risky."

"But you seem so optimistic in your book. You urge your readers to reach out for opportunities."

"But with caution. By all means trade your four duplexes if you're confident you can handle more, but project the new income conservatively—see that you have a safe cash-flow cushion to lean on. Trade for 20 or 30 apartments, but not for 120 in one jump. And remember what I said in my book, trade for a property when you see a chance to upgrade management so as to improve the cash flow, not for a property that's already well managed, 100 per cent occupied and priced to reflect it. Be sure you understand this very important point."

"You've convinced me not to make this trade. Can you offer any other advice as long as I have you on the phone?"

"Be sure to reconstruct operating statements that are submitted to you so they reflect what you consider the true annual rent, expenses, and cash flow. That's part of management expertise. If in doubt, call in an expert and get another opinion. Also, take a long look at the neighborhood. Is it changing? Try to project what it'll be like in five years from now, or ten years from now. Projecting the future tenancy potential is part of wise management. Buying or trading for a building is not like buying a washing machine or even a car. It's a much more important transaction. Tens of thousands of dollars are involved—how you retire, how gracefully you spend your golden years, depends on it. I'd better stop here. I don't want to talk up a big, long distance telephone bill for you."

"Don't worry. It's more than worth it. Thank you very much, and God bless you."

I didn't hear from the schoolteacher any further. I sincerely hope she didn't make the trade.

A NEW USE FOR AN OLD HOTEL

Old downtown hotels should never die, and unlike old generals they need not fade away.

A year ago, a real estate broker from Flint, Michigan, called and described a deal in his town that was one of those once-in-a-lifetime opportunities.

"A hotel that served our city for some 50 years," he was telling me, "has closed its doors because it was losing money. It couldn't compete with the new ones. Its owners renovated it a few years ago at a cost of a million dollars, but they still couldn't cut the mustard. Whether it was the new hotel competition or poor management is academic now—its owners want out. Would you go in with me on it? It's a sleeper. There's so much property and they're asking so little."

"I don't want to get involved in out-of-town property, but I'll be glad to talk to you about it."

"Here's what it's got—300 remodeled rooms, lots of public areas and in an 80 per cent downtown location."

"What can you get it for?"

"That's what's so exciting. I think I can buy it for $300,000, but it's got to be cash, and I haven't got it."

"It seems to me before buying it, you ought to have some idea what you're going to use it for."

"Well, that's why I'm calling you. I'd like to know how to put it to its best use and how to finance it. All I know now is that it's a bargain."

"Well, it does sound like a bargain, and here's a rough idea how you ought to proceed. First, the financing. Why don't you offer the owners of the hotel $400,000 instead of $300,000 providing they give you the following terms: $25,000 down and the balance of $375,000 at say $35,000 a year, including interest and principal, interest at 6 per cent. Tell them you will invest an additional $150,000 converting the 300 rooms into 150 efficiencies and small, one-bedroom apartments."

"I can handle the $25,000 down payment, but how do I raise the $150,000?"

"Reach for two angels high up in their income tax brackets. Then prepare a plan to lease one-third to permanent tenants, one-third to the elderly (including meals), and the remaining third to executives who prefer an apartment to a hotel when their housing needs extend into weeks or months. Construct an operating statement based on the use I describe. Offer your angels this deal: one-half interest, 90 per cent depreciation rights, and all of the cash flow to go to them for their $150,000 front money until it is repaid. Then they and you would be equal partners, sharing equally in equity and cash flow."

"Could you give me some idea as to what kind of remodeling I'd have to do?" my caller asked.

"The key word is converting—two small rooms into an efficiency, and two larger rooms into a one bedroom. All you do is remove walls between rooms and install kitchens in the extra bathrooms."

"Could you give me a rough idea what my monthly rental ought to be for the elderly with meals, weekly rental for executives, and the monthly rental for permanent tenants?"

"For senior citizens, with meals, $400 a month, for executives, $50 a week, and for permanent guests, $160 a month. This is what I'm getting in Milwaukee, and Flint, Michigan is probably in the same price range."

"You've been very patient and helpful. Is there anything else you can tell me before ending this very fruitful conversation?"

"Just one thing. If you should make your deal, don't forget to go to your city real estate assessor and show him what you paid for the hotel, so he can reassess it downward. Legitimately cutting your real estate taxes is like money in the bank."

"Thanks again." And he hung up.

I didn't hear from him again. In most cases, I don't. I share what I know and hope that the seeds of my suggestions bear fruit.

HOW A YOUNG MAN COULD EARN
$10,000 A YEAR FOR 30 YEARS

On a Sunday afternoon, a young man called me from Tallahassee, Fla. He began describing a 12,000-acre satellite tracking-station deal in the Bahamas. At first, I was skeptical. I thought someone was kidding me. But as the voice came across sincere, clear, and youthful, I began to concentrate on the very interesting problem he was posing across 2,000 miles of wire.

"I have the confidence of an elderly gentleman," he was saying, "who's in something of a financial bind in spite of owning a 12,000-acre farm in the Bahamas that he's leased for a satellite tracking-station to our government for 99 years at $100,000 a year."

"What's his problem?"

"He has a $750,000 mortgage on the tracking station farm from an English bank with payments of $100,000 a year including interest and principal, interest at 10 per cent. He not only has nothing left, but he has to pay income tax on the amortized principal which eats up all his other income. He'll have the farm free and clear in about 17 years, he told me, but in the meantime at age 65, he has little money to live on. How do I give him present income and make some money myself for arranging it?"

"Is the 99-year lease cancellable, and how many years has it to run?"

"Non-cancellable as far as I know, and it has 95 years left," came the triumphant reply.

"All right, here's the first thought that comes to my mind. Find a responsible buyer, have him assume the $750,000 mortgage with the $100,000 yearly payments, and for the owner's equity, have the buyer guarantee him $25,000 a year for 17 years, or during his lifetime, whichever is longer.

"To secure this $25,000 a year for the elderly owner, I'd insist that the buyer, who might be a corporation, guarantee this amount corporately and personally, and as an added precaution, that he buy an insurance policy naming the seller as beneficiary, the proceeds to guarantee the continuity of the $25,000-a-year income."

"Well, that takes care of the seller, and I'm glad you're so concerned about him, because he's got a great asset and I'd like to see him well taken care of. But now, why is this a good deal for the buyer?"

"It's an even better deal for the right buyer. First, he advances no cash as a down payment—only $25,000 a year for 17 years, or for your client's lifetime. That's a small price to pay for the remaining 80 years of a $100,000 annuity guaranteed by the U.S. Government."

"But in addition to paying $25,000 a year out of his pocket, the buyer would have to pay the income taxes that're now plaguing the owner."

"That's why I suggested a 'right' buyer who might have a loss carry forward or one who might create such a loss."

"Well, now that we've taken care of the buyer and seller, how do I fit into this? Since there's no cash passing hands, who'll take care of me?"

"How old are you?"

"Thirty-three."

"I've got a novel way for you to collect your fee. Listen carefully. You're entitled to a lot if you find the right buyer. Tell the owner that you don't want to touch his $25,000 a year, and tell the buyer, after he agrees to the deal, that you want $10,000 a year for 30 years, after the property is free and clear, and your buyer begins collecting $100,000 a year. You'll be 50 years old then, and a $10,000 yearly security for the next 30 years would be a nice thing to have. This arrangement would certainly please the seller, he's not paying it, and it'll please the buyer because the difference between getting $90,000 a year, and $100,000, 17 years from now, won't loom so big."

"You've been helpful and I'm grateful."

And on that friendly note our conversation ended.

A BOOKKEEPER GETS A LESSON
IN THE A B C'S OF REAL ESTATE INVESTING

What can a thirty-five year old career woman, earning $160 a week, do if she'd like to retire on a $15,000-a-year income? Tha question was put to me by a feminine-sounding bookkeeper working for an insurance company in Madison, Wisconsin.

"Your books are inspirational, full of hope," she enthused, "but most of your examples are beamed toward men. Could you offer some suggestions for a woman who likes her job, sees its financial limitations, but would nevertheless like to retire in middle-class style, say at $15,000 a year?"

"I'd like to answer your question with a success story that's as inspirational as it's practical. A German refugee couple with three small children came to Milwaukee after World War II, looking for a new life. While the husband was buffeted between unremunerative jobs and unsuccessful attempts to go into business for himself, his wife after learning enough English, bought a duplex from an owner who wanted to get rid of management problems. He wasn't as interested in the down payment as in someone who was reliable. She turned out to be very reliable. Using this experience as a credential, she found another unsatisfied duplex owner and bought it the same way she acquired the first one. Then she went further. She alerted a dozen brokers to her reliability and ability to manage small properties. Within five years she owned a dozen duplexes, and by the time her eldest daughter graduated from the University of Wisconsin, the refugee mother was clearing about $15,000 a year and living in a fashionable suburb. She didn't expand beyond that (she was getting older), but with the little her husband earned, they educated their three children, and the family rose into the middle class. The point of the story is that you, with your education, have an even better chance to do what she did—providing you have a feel for it."

"But how do I get started," she asked after listening to my dissertation.

"First, learn all you can about managing small properties. There are all kinds of management materials, as well as adult management courses in real estate. When you feel you're ready, go to your city hall and copy names of property owners in areas you're interested in. Write several hundred letters that begin something like this: 'If you're looking for someone reliable to sell your property to, I could be the one. I don't have a lot of money, but if you sell your (duplex, four-family, whatever) to me, you can count on getting your payments promptly and regularly!'

"And you need not stop there. Visit a dozen brokers the way the refugee woman did and tell them your story—that you're looking for trouble property with small down payments. You may hear within a week, a month or a year. Be patient—opportunity may come when you least expect it. When it does, act promptly. If it's an unusually good deal and you don't have enough money for a down payment—get an investor angel—show him how he can make money by buying it with you."

"How? Can you give me an example?"

"Well, suppose there's an old four-family for sale for $50,000, and you feel it's an excellent buy, but you don't have the $10,000 down payment to buy it. And no one will loan you the $10,000 because you have no collateral. Then find a friend, a relative, or business acquaintance and explain the profitability of the deal. Offer a half-partnership for the down payment with the carrot that the first cash flow money goes to pay off the $10,000. If your deal has enough overage after fixed expenses and mortgage payments to pay it off in four years—it's an extraordinary deal, and it gets less extraordinary with each additional year. And when it reaches ten years, it's no good.

"I've thrown a lot of ideas at you. If your mind is tuned to this kind of thinking, you'll do well. If you lack judgment in these matters, you'll give up. But don't be downhearted—you still have your bookkeeping. Give these ideas a try for a couple of years—by that time, you'll know if you're cut out for it."

"I'm glad I called. Keep on writing books, Mr. Bockl, we need people like you to prod us on."

BEFORE YOU PLUNGE AFTER BIG MONEY, GET YOUR FEET WET IN LITTLE MONEY

Anyone who's after big money before learning how to make any money, is making a big mistake. Often it can nip a promising real estate career in the bud.

A young man called from Kentucky one day and asked point blank how to skip the small piddling deals and plunge directly into making big money.

"I'm a college graduate, I majored in finance and I work for a bank," he said crisply. "But they're too darned conservative here. I've read your books and I like your wide vision, your leverage ideas that build fortunes. I'm in a hurry. I don't want to waste ten years piddling around with small stuff. I want big action and big money right away."

"Hold on, young man," I cautioned sternly. "You've got the wrong idea about leverage. You use it only when you've analyzed, researched, and taken every precaution that the stream of income will be larger than total expenses, and not for one year, but for the foreseeable future. How can you do that without any experience?"

"But I don't want to get into the rut of small-time experience. For instance, I have a chance to go in with someone to sell mobile homes to foreign countries. I can buy repossessed homes for $4,000 apiece and sell them for $6,000 in Nicaragua. If I sell a hundred, I can make $200,000."

"Are you familiar with the Nicaraguan foreign exchange? Do you know if there's an import tax that could wipe out your profit? Do you sell to the government or a private party? And how sure are you of getting your money after your sale?"

"I don't know the answers to your questions."

"Then don't go into it. You don't jump into eight feet of water if you don't know how to swim."

"Well I suppose you're right, but here's another idea that tantalizes me. In your *Fortune* book, you discuss the conduit idea—a young man buying property from an elderly owner and paying him out of profits. There's a 65-year-old cement-block manufacturer who wants me to take over his business. He's tired and wants out. He's asking $250,000. His equipment alone, he says, is worth $250,000, and he's willing to sell it to me with practically nothing down. Isn't that a leveraging opportunity?"

"I don't know. What was his average profit the last three years?"

"About $10,000 a year, but that's becaase he wasn't trying, he says."

"And how does he want you to pay off the $250,000?"

"At the rate of $25,000 a year."

"And where will the $25,000 come from?"

"From an increase in business."

"Since you don't know anything about manufacturing and selling cement blocks, how are you going to increase business. Getting into deals with little money is a prescription for failure if you haven't the faintest idea where the stream of income is coming from. I'm afraid your international mobile-home sales idea and paying off $25,000 a year to the cement-block manufacturer out of increased business, are both pipe dreams. My advice is to hold on to your bank job and try little things—like buying a duplex or four-family, and learn all you can about real estate management. From the way you talk, you need a lot of seasoning. Undisciplined ambition is like a wild mare. Tame it before you ride it."

"I get the point. Thank you for taking time to cool me off. I still intend to get to the top, but I better do it slowly."

A PRACTICAL SUGGESTION
ON TRADING YOURSELF OUT OF A DILEMMA

The phone was ringing just as I completed 20 minutes of my transcendental meditation.

"My name is Hollingsworth and I'm calling you from Atlanta, Georgia." His thick Southern drawl was slow and pleasant.

"What can I do for you, Mr. Hollingsworth?" I asked.

"I've read your books and I think you might be the man to get me out of the bind I'm in."

"What is it?"

"I've been a successful land developer for a dozen years. Now in 1975, I find myself with a million dollars worth of good land bucking $500,000 of short-term bank financing. As long as I met my obligations, my banker was the friendliest man you'd ever want to meet, but now he's grown hostile. I'm in this kind of a fix. I can't build—there's no market. I can't sell the land—nobody wants it. I can't meet the bank's notes—no one else will loan me the money. What do I do?"

"Is the land really worth a million dollars? Or is it just your figure?"

"Ten years of hard work have gone into the equity of this land. Two years ago, I could have sold it in a day for a million. It's prime land, ready for building as soon as things open up."

"And you stand to lose it all unless you pay the bank's obligations?"

"I'm afraid so."

"What would you like to get out of it?"

"First, I don't want to go bankrupt. That's what the bank is threatening. Second, if I could get a third or even a fifth of what I've got in it, I'd be satisfied."

"Then here's what I suggest you do. Compose an ad reading something like this:

> WILL TRADE
> my $500,000 equity in improved land for any income property. Land suitable for condominiums, singles and apartments. Must exchange at once. Land will surely increase in value if you can hold it for five years.

Show this ad to your banker so he stops breathing down your neck. Explain to him that you're looking for someone with income property who is paying half of the net to the government. Explain to the banker that if the buyer you're searching for makes the trade and pays off $100,000 toward the $500,000 balance, he can use the interest he has to pay on the $400,000 plus the real estate taxes on the land as deductions against his other income. In the meantime, the land's value will be enhanced and in five years he could quadruple what he used as a down payment to trade for the land."

"You're not exaggerating," Hollingsworth interrupted. "Anyone who trades with me would be making a killing. I wish I could find a way to wait it out myself, so I could make the killing."

"But the bank won't wait five years. I suggest you try the ad in several metropolitan newspapers, hopefully winding up with a free and clear 12-family, rather than facing bankruptcy."

"Any other ideas?"

"Well, if you could find an investing angel to advance a couple of hundred thousand to your impatient banker for a half equity in your land, that wouldn't be bad either. That should satisfy your creditor. I'm sure he'd be willing to wait for the balance until the land ripens for sale or use. This could be a bonanza for the angel. And as for you, a half-a-loaf is better than no loaf."

"You've given me two practical ideas, and I'm going to give each my immediate attention."

"And you might add," I said, "push both ideas simultaneously—that's how you increase your chances of success."

"I'm extremely grateful. Thank you for your time and interesting suggestions."

NO KIDDING—SOMEONE BOUGHT A MISSISSIPPI BRIDGE

I couldn't believe it, but a call came in one afternoon from an attorney in Lansing, Michigan, asking me if his client ought to consummate the purchase of a Mississippi bridge.

"I'm not facetious, Mr. Bockl," he said seriously. "My client and I have read your books, and she suggested I call you."

"O.K., if you're serious, I'll try to be serious too."

"My client is a widow. Her husband was a sort of promoter, and before he died, he put a $35,000 down payment on the purchase of a bridge across the Mississippi for $150,000. Now my client is uncertain whether to drop the down payment or go ahead with the deal. Her husband's idea was to build a restaurant and shops on the bridge, much like they do over highways. It's close to a highly traveled road and there's ample parking on either side. It's not such a looney idea. What do you think?"

"Do you have a feasibility study for this project?"

"No. I've checked into it, and they want $15,000."

"Can the widow get her $35,000 down payment back?"

"I don't know yet."

"Here's what I think. First, I would definitely not spend the $15,000 for a feasibility report, and second, try to get back as much of the $35,000 as you can."

"I take it then, you're not for the project."

"Certainly not, especially for a widow. It's too bizarre. It may take years before it gets off the ground—by that time, she could be wiped out. I'd recommend it for a wealthy man as a fun deal, or for a promotionally minded entrepreneur with financial staying power, but not for your client. It's way too risky."

"I tend to agree with you. While there's more to it than buying the Brooklyn Bridge, still, as you say, it's too bizarre. Thank you for your time and advice. I'm sure my client will appreciate it."

7

How to Use Time to Ripen
Real Estate Into a Fortune

Some men know how to read real estate signs and predict the future. They make millions. Their prognostications are a mixture of ingenuity, logic and patience.

A LITTLE GUY TACKLES A FINANCIAL GIANT—AND WINS

Maury Abbot, a young entrepreneur, read the signs right and bought a worn out, 24-family apartment building next to the largest insurance company in the city, and waited—waited until its need for more parking would become so acute that it would be ready to pay almost any price for the adjacent site.

Let's begin 15 years ago when a lawyer bought the 24-family for $105,000. It was a shambles. After a few years, he got tired of it and sold it to Maury for $150,000, even though it was showing a 12 per cent return. But it was a troublesome property and the $45,000 profit looked good. Young Abbot, however, saw another dimension in the deal. If he could maintain even a 7 per cent return with cosmetic repairs for five or ten years, his killing would come when the property would be ready for razing, when the insurance company needed it badly.

In 1973, 42-year-old Maury was approached by a broker. Would he like to sell his 24-family apartment building? He had a gut feeling the broker was representing the next-door insurance company.

"Yes," he said. "I'll sell."

"How much?"

"Five hundred thousand dollars!"

"You must be kidding."

"I'm not kidding. I've suffered with this property for ten long years. Managing it was no picnic. Now that the insurance company wants it, it'll have to pay for all the headaches it gave me.'"

"How do you know it's an insurance company that's interested?"

"Come on, let's not play any games."

"O.K. I'll admit it, but we know what you paid for it, and $500,000 is exorbitant."

"I don't think so. This property was offered to the insurance company before I bought it. It didn't want to bother with the troublesome tenants because it didn't need the land. Now it needs it. Well, I want to be paid for my patience, my troubles and my foresight."

"Will you take $350,000?"

"I'm afraid it will have to be $500,000."

"But if we don't buy it, you couldn't get $250,000 for it. We're offering you $100,000 for all your patience and vision. Isn't that enough?"

"Let's look at it from the insurance company's standpoint," Abbot said. "If it can't get this property for parking, the value of its office building could suffer by $1,000,000, maybe more. Its employees are now parking blocks away, and I know they don't like it. This lot will bring the work force close to their work—a valuable amenity. In fact, it's a must—even if your company had to pay $750,000. Right?"

"You drive a hard bargain."

"I don't think so. You're buying a very valuable piece of land. It can't be duplicated. There's only one such piece. It's unique. You know it. And what's more important, I know it."

The insurance company paid the $500,000. The multi-billion dollar company wasn't interested in bothering with marginal property when it didn't need it—and paid a high price for it.

But this game of buying and waiting is not for the real estate illiterate. If you don't know how to read the signs, it can be disastrous.

RUN A RESTAURANT AND LET THE SURROUNDING 20 ACRES GROW INTO A FORTUNE

There's a beautiful restaurant on the outskirts of Milwaukee, nestled amidst 20 lovely wooded acres overlooking Lake Michigan, which 15 years from now could become a plush condominium project with the gourmet dining room as its centerpiece. This is no ordinary restaurant or ordinary site. A lifetime of creative effort went into the chalet-like building and gourmet menu. The ravined land is not zoned for condominiums yet, but residential growth is pointing in its direction, and in a decade it is destined to ripen into a prime, exclusive living area.

The father who poured 25 years into this project died, and his son is not interested in continuing where the father left off. It's for sale, and what an opportunity for someone to run the restaurant and wait for the land to ripen into a fortune. The son is meeting sales resistance because prospective buyers are only looking at the bottom line of the restaurant's operations, and not at the site's developmental potential. And since the bottom line is dangerously close to red ink, the $400,000 the son is asking turns people away.

After several meetings with the son, I suggested that he structure a sale as follows: Have the buyer assume the outstanding $225,000 first mortgage, take a $25,000 down payment, and arrange for a second mortgage of $150,000 to be amortized over 20 years at 8 per cent. That would make the buyer's debt service on the first and second mortgages about $40,000 a year, a stiff payment, but manageable because it's one of Wisconsin's outstanding restaurants. When the father ran it, its volume was close to $1,000,000 a year. It is now down to $200,000.

It so happens that I have a young man who is ready to buy the property on the terms I suggested. He's ready to "tough" it out for the next ten years because he sees the land's subdividing future. He sees, as I see, the time when the sale of the land could pay off the outstanding mortgages and leave his restaurant free and clear in the midst of a luxury planned development with the gourmet-minded neighbors adding a boost to his food and drink volume.

But the young seller, so far, is adamant about his cash demands even though he's flirting with foreclosure. He's shortsightedly looking for a restaurant buyer with $175,000 in cash, and they're as difficult to find as a black cat sleeping in a dark room.

Sooner or later the impasse will be resolved—sooner if he follows my advice and gets a $150,000 second mortgage out of the deal, and later if he gambles for the cash and finds that it's too late to get anything.

Of course, reading the signs without having a definite plan in mind, is meaningless. It won't make any sense. That's why I keep stressing new approaches to old problems. They light up the imagination with new ideas, and the result could be a work of financial art—fascinating and profitable.

BUY A FARM NEAR A HIGHWAY
AND WAIT FOR THE HARVEST TO COME IN

Five years ago, a German immigrant, who had become my friend, came to my office and said:

"You've been kind to me and I want to reciprocate. A friend of mine from the old country who's along in years, wants to sell his 180-acre farm. I know you'll see to it that he gets the right price. Also you might have some unusual idea for the land."

I thanked him for his good will and we drove off to see the farm. My pulse quickened as my mind soaked up the peaceful environment of old world sturdiness—the 100-year-old gray farmhouse, the animal smell of the barn, the whitewashed milkhouse, the horse corral. Although we were only 15 minutes from the city, the rural impact was so absorbingly quiet, that for a few moments I was held in its spell—except for two jarring distractions—the hum of freeway automobiles to the left, and the snaking lines of railroad tracks to the right. I had to wrench myself out of my nostalgic mood to get my commercial wheels turning.

What an opportunity for a young man, I ruminated as I was driving home. The farm was still too far away in miles and years for commercial building—but not so far off for someone who is young in years, has a love for the soil and an eye for the future. The farm was perfectly located to provide an ideal homestead for a young couple with a lot of children who liked to dabble in farming while the little ones were growing up, but would know what to do with the land when the children flew the coop.

The farmer was asking $175,000—in cash. He was from the old school and I knew that the conduit idea, low interest rates and long amortization would only confuse him. He even resisted giving me a listing—he wanted no obligations.

The couple I had in mind for the farm was a young lawyer with his wife and three children. I knew they would jump at the chance of restoring old buildings and waiting 20 years for the land to ripen while their children roamed the acres in healthy, country living. But how many young families have $175,000 in cash?

I did some thinking. I knew I couldn't budge the farmer, nor did I want to. I also knew that the young lawyer had a longing for land, but little cash. I described the farm to him and projected its future potential—a possible industrial park, a shopping center, home development, apartment development, etc. My young attorney friend was captiviated with the double-pronged advantages—20 years of rural living capped with a money harvest at the end of it.

After he viewed the farm, his desire rose to white heat. "If you can figure out a way for me to own it, I'd be eternally grateful."

"How much could you put together in cash if you really tried?"

"If I really tried—about $25,000."

"How much do you earn a year?"

"About $20,000."

"What do you think you could earn off the land?"

"If the sale price included the 15 milk cows and his farm equipment, I could put a man on the land and perhaps eke out another $7,500."

"Do you know anyone who likes you and likes money as well?"

"Well, let's see. There's a wealthy member of our law firm who likes me—and I'm sure he likes money too."

"Here's my plan. Have your wealthy colleague co-sign a $150,000 mortgage on the farm and make half the $15,000-a-year payment to the lender, and get credit for it in the form of a cumulative second mortgage from you to him, let's say for 15 years. At the end of that period you'd owe him $112,500. In addition agree to give him half interest in the farm. You see, you don't have enough income to qualify for a $150,000 mortgage. You need an angel."

"Let's see." He thought for awhile. "I want it so badly I think I would do it. He'd be getting a hell of a good deal."

"I know, but only if he's getting a hell of a good deal will he do it."

I explained the deal to the young attorney's angel.

"If you have confidence in your associate, your exposure would be minimal compared to the bonanza you'd be getting at the end of 15 years."

"Yes," he said, "I'd be interested. But only because I like him. If it were anyone else, I'd pass it—even though the terms are generous in my favor."

I made a few inquiries about a $150,000 mortgage backed by the young attorney's signature and co-signed by his angel. Several lending agencies turned me down. They found the arrangement too unorthodox. But one savings-and-loan association said yes. I called the farmer.

"I can get $175,000 in cash for your farm. I have it all arranged."

"I'm sorry," he said. "I've sold it. I took a deposit several days ago."

I was diasppointed, but not as disappointed as the young attorney who had his heart set on it. I failed, but I have taken the time to explain my failure in the hope that buying a farm, enjoying it, and reaping a harvest of real estate growth, may trigger an idea in your mind. And the financing plan may also appeal to you, if you're short of cash and long on dreams.

SATELLITE LAND CAN RIPEN INTO A FORTUNE

In Wisconsin as in other states, resorts are often located near small towns. Many such vacation spots have hundreds of acres surrounding the resort buildings. Some of this extra land may be wooded, a golf course along a river, or beside a lake. With the anticipated growth of small towns, this extra land could ripen for subdividing 10 or 15 years from now.

Many medium-sized towns, and even small ones, are developing shopping centers on the outskirts at the confluence or well-traveled highways. As soon as such plans are announced, or if you want to play it safe, as soon as you see that the shopping center is going to be successful, buy a tract of nearby land for future satellite development.

An astute man in a good-sized city read the real estate signs correctly when a regional shopping center was proposed about ten miles from town. He bought a mile of frontage at less than $50 a front foot across the highway and waited. Two years later when the shopping center was completed, prospects began offering him $100 a foot. He turned them down. Three years later when the center gained its initial momentum, he had offers of $150 a foot and still he held on. Five years later when the center ripened into a success, his satellite land was in demand at $500 a foot. He started selling—a few parcels a year—and when he was through, his foresight, patience, and timing netted him more profit than the $20,000,000 shopping center earned in its first ten years of operations.

And remember, it all started with an investment of $250,000!

But what about the smaller investor—one who has $10,000 to $25,000 to invest? There are opportunities for him too. Look around. If you see a neglected mansion on a big lot in a small town— investigate it. The chances are that a widow is rattling alone in the big house, or it's an estate bringing in a low rental. If you have a big family, buy the big house, move into it and let the land grow in value. At a later date, have the parcel rezoned into an apartment site, at which time developers may pay from $4,000 to $5,000 per unit for land. By that time, your children will probably have grown to college age, and the profit will come in handy for their education.

Or you may spot an empty lot, a house, or a neglected piece of commercial property near a bank or public utility building. If you can buy it at a price at which the income will pay the fixed expenses and debt service, grab it. And even if you have to take a little money from "home" every year, hold on to it. Five, ten, fifteen years from now, you'll be glad you did. You'll be in the path of growth, and rewarded for your foresight and patience with a hefty profit.

Of course, a corner tract of land at the junction of two highly travelled roads is always a prudent risk, if the terms are right—that's more important than price. If you're a doctor, lawyer or anyone in a high income bracket who can tie up such a corner for, let's say, $165,000 with $15,000 down and pay interest and real estate taxes for 15 years, the government will pick up half the tab through reduced income taxes. Then when your income subsides in 15 years, the land should be ripe for selling. The corner could become valuable for a gasoline station or a savings-and-loan company, and the rest of the land could be zoned residential or commercial, depending on the general community plans.

A note of warning. There's always such a thing as buying a "dead horse," or a future that is beyond your life span. I know of a young man who bought a mountain slope for $250,000 near Phoenix, Arizona, and waited 20 years. Nothing happened. He's 60 years old now and the mountain goats are still roaming its craggy heights. Another man bought a mountain near Tucson, Arizona, when he was 30, and after tiring of paying interest and taxes for ten years, sold it at a huge loss.

Obviously, buying real estate for future growth is a risky business. It requires a lot of study and a bit of intuition. Or a lot of intuition, if there are no facts to study. Whatever combination you use, you'll never eliminate the element of risk. But that's part of the fun. Just think how drab life would be if you knew all the answers in advance. Well-managed uncertainty is the spice of life.

SEVEN WAYS TO USE TIME PROFITABLY

The popular adage "time is money," barely begins to suggest the importance of time. Time is like a commodity which you begin using as soon as you're born. Only when you believe in reincarnation does time stretch into eternity. But as far as your present incarnation is concerned, here is the way to use time to the best advantage in building a yearly income in investment real estate

1. Let time work for you. Start buying investment property as early as possible. If you start at 50 instead of 25, you may have lost a fortune. Don't use the alibi that it's difficult to get money when you're young. Use the various approaches described in this book to overcome the money problem. By planting early your investment has more time to grow to harvest.

2. Time can work against you too—if you use poor judgment. A doctor friend of mine built a 10,000 sq. ft. medical clinic for $225,000 about 15 years ago. He moved his own office into it and leased some 90 per cent of the space to other doctors. Then the neighborhood changed drastically. The doctor had little knowledge or time to cope with the new conditions. His occupancy plummeted to 50 per cent. He sold his $225,000 investment for $100,000, and leased space in another building. Instead of doubling his investment as others had done during the same 15-year period, my friend's was cut in half. In his case, time worked against him.

3. *There is a time to buy and a time to sell.* When you're 30 you buy for the future, and when you're 65 you sell to enjoy a leisurely present.

4. *What should you do when you're 45?* You are about 20 years away from selling, and have missed 20 years of buying? With the savings you have accumulated by now, you should accelerate your buying program. But don't get trapped with a short amortization period resulting in big monthly payments. This is a time when you need all the cash flow you can get to support children in school, a bigger apartment, or a more expensive home.

5. *What if you're 65 and in good health?* Should you cash in your chips and do nothing? Absolutely not! Convert your properties to land contracts or cash for your security, and take on a few interesting projects, but with exculpatory clauses in your borrowing to limit your personal liability. Under no circumstances should you jeopardize your security. Practice your accumulated real estate wisdom, but don't gamble with your retirement income.

6. *When your depreciation lines cross, trade.* That is, when your depreciation benefits are beginning to thin out, don't sell, this is a time to trade. Here is why. When you sell, hopefully at a profit, you'll be paying a huge chunk in taxes. When you trade, and be sure you're trading up, not down, you not only avoid taxes but you get a new and higher depreciation base. Be sure to talk this over with your accountant or tax attorney to time your trade so you get all the benefits you're entitled to.

7. Sell or trade your real estate when you see that your neighborhood is deteriorating. First, you should make every attempt to upgrade the neighborhood and your property, but if you can't get cooperation, and the surrounding real estate begins to look shabby—don't wait until your property remains the best in the block. That's too late. The other neglected properties will drag yours down. The right timing of your move could involve thousands of dollars. Watch it—carefully!

8

Creating New Uses for Old Buildings Is the Real Estate Bonanza Of the Future

One of my pupils, an electrician with no real estate skills whatsoever, earned the equivalent of $1,000,000 in one year because he used the simple yet revolutionary real estate principle of increasing cash flow through skillful management.

His self-created project is an inspirational lesson in building a big continuing yearly income which even some sophisticated investors are not fully aware of. Here is his astounding story.

MERCHANDIZING THE CHARM OF AN OLD THEATER BUILDING CREATES A $50,000 YEARLY INCOME

A multi-million dollar, New York based, movie-theater chain owned a 2,000-seat theater property with seven attached stores, a 16-lane basement bowling alley, and a 100x120 vacant parking lot a few blocks away. The top echelon owners of the property had probably never seen the inside of the theater. If they had, they probably saw only the dust covered oriental figurines of the high domed ceiling, and the grimy plastered ornamentation of the lobby. What they did see clearly, was the red on the bottom line, and they instructed one of their underlings to get rid of it. But there are few buyers for real estate that's losing money—unless someone sees a hidden potential.

My pupil, let's call him Al, saw what the New York owners didn't—the beauty that lay under the dust and grime inside the old theater. He offered the owners $275,000 with $25,000 down and the balance of $250,000 in cash in 18 months. They hesitated, waited for other offers, and when none came, accepted it. Al then borrowed $75,000 from his bank and began infusing new life into the old building.

He cement-pebbled the front of the stores, and by creating a new image, he was able to raise the rent of three stores and fill the four vacant ones. The 6,000 square feet of space above the stores had been vacant for years. He painted it, installed new vinyl flooring and electrical fixtures, and leased it at $2 a square foot. The cavernous basement was a catchall for the building's junk—a sorry environment for the few bowlers who patronized the forlorn lanes. He painted, paneled and fixtured the vacant part of the basement into a nightclub bar. Both the bar and the bowling business soon spurted into a profitable activity.

The lot that came with the deal was a loser for the previous owner. It was vacant because no one took the time to lease it. Al did. He canvassed the neighborhood and filled it with day and night parkers for a $9000-a-year revenue.

But the big bonanza was the theater. The owners ran it as a third-rate movie house with third-rate results. However, the new owner had other ideas. With the sensitivity that is necessary in restoring a beautiful antique, Al plunged into removing the years of neglect. What he found beneath the layers of grimy dust, was a treasure of art—Chinese, Persian, Indian and Thai sculpture and paintings upon which the original builders had lavished huge sums of money. The theater was reputed to have cost $1,500,000 in 1925.

Al had a problem. The bid to repaint the plastered ornamentation of six larger-than-life Buddhist idols, 26 dragons standing on elephant heads, several dozen peacocks and thousands of silver, gold, green and red polychrome designs was shockingly high—

$35,000. Al solved that by buying a special paint from some firm in Tennessee for $1,500. His wife and son painted the lower part of the theater, while he catwalked and bronzed the high domed areas.

The three huge chandeliers in the lobby were handmade in Thailand, but looked like worn-out junk. The 900 bulbs were dirt laden and most of them were burned out. Al hand-restored the chandeliers and replaced the bulbs. The result was three beautiful bouquets of light that brightened every nook and cranny of the newly decorated and carpeted foyer.

When he was through, the City Landmarks Commission designated it as a City Landmark—an honor given only to unusual buildings. A half dozen stories appeared in the local newspapers. An architectural historian eloquently described it as the most artistic temple of oriental art to be found in America, and a theater buff described the stage as the most elaborate in Wisconsin.

What did all this do for Al and his theater? A lot! He began getting requests for special events from the two urban universities, several music organizations, children's theater groups, and for special movie runs. The big company lost money in the theater, but Al made it to the tune of $25,000 a year after all expenses. Two years after Al took hold of the project, he was clearing $50,000.00 a year, after debt service on a new $350,000 mortgage. He used the proceeds to pay off the $250,000 balance to the owners and the $75,000 he borrowed from the bank for remodeling.

Just think of it! With no money of his own, he created a yearly income that the average man can only dream about. Yet, here was an average man who did it, and so easily, because he knew how to merchandize the charm and function of an old building. It's a financial miracle—an ordinary man earning the equivalent of a million dollars in less than two years!

Yet, that's exactly what happened.

CONVERTING A 120-YEAR-OLD FACTORY BUILDING INTO 174 APARTMENTS

When a 120-year-old factory building is converted into 174 apartments—that is electrifying real estate news. There have been few such conversions in the country. That's why my curiosity was aroused when I received a note from one of my readers, telling me that 174 families are now living in modern apartments, in what used to be a piano factory more than a century ago, in Boston, Mass. It's the story of a dead building resurrected to life.

There are literally tens of thousands of multi-story factory buildings that have been abandoned by industry for one-story industrial parks, and most of them are either vacant or put to their lowest use—storage. With apartment construction costs sky high, it behooves us to take a long look at the feasibility of converting industrial buildings into residential living quarters.

The Boston five-story, block long, 250,000 square foot factory was built in 1853. After more than a century of industrial use, it will now be home for people paying $91 a month for 500 square feet, up to $400 a month for apartments of 1700 square feet. The people occupying these apartments cover a wide range too. They're a mixture of artists, craftsmen, dancers, writers, musicians, photographers, and architects.

One of the reasons for this artistic potpourri is that one of the building's four wings has been set aside—about 30,000 square feet—exclusively as work space for the tenants at a pittance rental. And an added attraction is an interior landscaped 22,500 square feet of open space courtyard, designed with various amenities for relaxing, reading, and for playground and cultural activities.

The conversion to apartments cost $10 a square foot, and this was accomplished by retaining much of the old charm—ceilings, beams, stairways—wherever possible. In many places for example, the floors needed patching. The patches show—but they have the class of an old tweed jacket with patched elbows.

What was successfully done in Boston, can be duplicated anywhere in the U.S. where there's an acute demand for housing. Let's take a typical multi-story factory building in any typical city and follow it through step by step from buying, converting and operating it after it's changed to residential use.

First, the neighborhood must be suited for residential use. Second, the building should be soundly constructed, preferably of steel and concrete. Thirdly, a long rectangular building is better suited to remodeling than a square one. Obviously a building with a typical floor plan of 60 x 175 or 10,500 square feet lends itself more readily to conversion than a 100 x 100 floor plan with a lot of inner dark space.

Assuming you've found a 60 x 175 concrete, five-story factory building in a fair neighborhood—what should you pay for it? Not more than $3 a square foot, or about $150,000. Two dollars a square foot or $100,000 would be a lot safer. You've got to get a bargain because you're engaged in unorthodox remodeling, and the safer you play it, the more you can cushion your mistakes.

By providing a six-foot corridor across the length of the building with some indentations to break up the monotony, you'd have about 27 feet from corridor to window. The typical one-bedroom apartment could be about 27 x 27 or a little over 700 square feet. That would give you an approximate 15 x 16 living room and a 12 x 12 bedroom each facing the windows, and room for a bathroom, kitchen, dinette, closet and storage area on the inside. Subtracting about 1,500 square feet for hallways, wall thickness, stairwells and elevator shafts, would leave about 9,000 net livable square feet per floor, divided by 700, or 13 apartments.

Five floors of 13 apartments would create a rent roll of 65 times $160 for a one-bedroom apartment per month, or about $125,000 per year—less 7 per cent for vacancies—rounded out to $116,000 net. Assuming 40 per cent for fixed expenses, or $46,400 (a general rule of thumb percentage), would leave $116,000 less $46,400, or close to $70,000 before debt service. Remodeling 50,000 square feet at $10 a square foot would cost $500,000. Assuming you could procure a mortgage for $500,000 at 9 1/2 per cent for 25 years, the debt service would be about $55,000 a year, leaving you a cash flow of $70,000 less $55,000, or $15,000 a year for your $150,000 investment—the original cost of the factory building.

Not a good deal. You're entitled to a lot more for your effort. And I presume that's why few factory buildings are converted into residential living quarters. But if you could have bought the building for $50,000, then it would have been an excellent deal. That's why these factory buildings must be bought at bargain prices.

If the neighborhood is good, if the demand for apartments is strong, if you have the ingenuity to convert for $10 a square foot or less, if you find a lender who is sympathetic to the conservation principle—then by all means look into the feasibility of recycling factory buildings into functional apartments. In addition to creating a yearly income, you'll have the fun of pioneering a new type of conversion.

And you'll get special merit in conservation too.

A CLOSE LOOK AT THE VARIETY OF OPPORTUNITIES IN CHANGING OLD BUILDINGS TO NEW USES

Because of fast-changing economic and social conditions, users of buildings not only have the problem of physical obsolescence, but use obsolescence; that is, sound buildings no longer meeting present needs. That's why finding new uses for old properties has become one of the most profitable sectors of the real estate profession. It is especially true today, when it's becoming more and more difficult to show a profit in new construction due to astronomical building costs and two-digit interest rates.

With the help of the National Association of Realtors, of which I'm a member, I'd like to share some unusual conversion ideas in the hope they may trigger action in your own community.

It makes better economic sense, for instance, to convert a vacant fraternity or sorority house into an eight-family than to build a new eight-family. A lessening of interest in fraternities and sororities provides opportunities to buy them at bargain prices. A variation is to convert the old "frats" into foster homes under the welfare program.

In Fort Collins, Colorado, a church was remodeled and leased to the State Government for an employment office. Another church was changed to a studio for production of training films. And still another was bought by the Salvation Army for its headquarters.

Abandoned gasoline stations offer profitable opportunities for creative conversions. First, they can be bought at bargain prices. Second, they're usually in good corner locations and lend themselves to a variety of uses. Here are a few: a small restaurant, a liquor store, real estate office, florist shop, travel agency, photo shop, cleaning establishment, and if you put your mind to it, I'm sure you can come up with others.

A small motel on a by-passed highway need not remain a loser. It can be used for manufacturers' "reps," one-man insurance agents, small repair shops, showroom marts, doctors' clinics, rehabilitation centers, nursing homes, or small furnished apartments.

Outmoded car dealership buildings in congested areas not only lend themselves to offices, as noted elsewhere, but to fine restaurants, furniture showrooms, hardware stores, and recreation centers for young people.

Penney's Gambles, A & P, and stores of a similar nature, are changing their merchandizing methods. They're abandoning small stores for super stores. That's where you come in. These small but sound buildings can be converted to a variety of uses—offices, mini-malls, restaurants, medical clinics and mini-theaters.

What do you do with a five-story, 300-car parking structure that's losing money? Well, if you don't have any ideas, you sell it. That's what a Chicago owner did—at one-third it's cost—to an entrepreneur who had an idea.

He developed it in several stages. First, he converted part of the ground floor's 20,000 square feet into three stores—a jewelry shop, a gift store, and a nationally known car-rental office He then changed the former high-priced pick up and delivery parking service, which employed five runners, to a low priced, self-parking system run by one employee. Within a few months, the operation began making money.

But the new owner didn't stop there. He built a mall in the remaining first floor space and leased stores to a furrier, a ballroom accessory business, a bookstore owner and men's apparel proprietor. Soon after, the entrepreneur checked the feasibility of converting the second floor parking to retail space.

The car-rental firm on the first floor was doing so well, it leased the top floor for storage of its cars. That gave the owner an idea. He leased the two remaining floors for new-car storage to another tenant. The ingenious man has no employees on the premises now, and you can use your own imagination how well he's doing compared to the previous owner who was running a losing parking business in a building that outlived its original use.

If residential real estate can be condominiumized, why not a huge factory building? That's just what happened in Southfield, Michigan, when a 350,000 square foot factory building couldn't be sold because it was too big for most buyers. A creative entrepreneur bought it, and condominiumized it to a half-dozen buyers. It was a case of divide and conquer. There were no buyers when it was offered as one large unit, but there were plenty of buyers when it was subdivided into smaller ones.

A DEPRESSED AREA IS REVITALIZED BY NEW IDEAS

In Toronto, Canada, converting old properties to new uses has revitalized a depressed area of seven blocks.

One was a three-story building with 9,000 square feet on each floor. It had four ramshackle stores on the first floor, a printer on the second, and storage on the third. The new owners gutted the entire inside of the building and put on a new outside facade with the word MARKET prominently displayed across it. The interior was changed into a miniature merchandise mart. Each floor was divided into 50 selling stalls, each stand about 10 x 10 which the tenant could decorate with an awning, blind or anything that suited his or her fancy. Thus a prospective customer could browse through 150 little shops offering items such as odd-lot shoes, linen, bath towels, antiques, old coins, Italian cheeses, etc.

The value of this building has doubled from $400,000 to $800,000. And the entrepreneur deserves every dollar of it because he's done something novel. He risked prudently and was rewarded magnificently.

The other project which vivified the depressed area was even more unusual. An innovative "redeveloper" bought seven old buildings with a total rentable area of 146,000 square feet. They were used for dead storage, bringing from 80 to 90 cents a square foot, and most of the space was vacant. The courageous entrepreneur converted them into—believe it or not—a stage theater, studios, a global village theater for youth, manufacturing of science productions company, an old Bavarian restaurant, a concession store, a discotheque, an art gallery, a framing studio, etc. Where the previous owners had difficulty getting 80 cents a square foot, the creative owner was now getting $2 a square foot. What's equally important, is that in addition to increasing income from a trickle to a steady stream, new life was breathed into old buildings and a depressed area was revitalized. It's an excellent example of how the profit motive and conservation can join hands to form a mutually beneficial partnership.

FROM SAFEWAY STORE TO SCHOOL

The possibilities of converting old buildings to new uses are endless. In Colorado Springs, an imaginative convertor bought a Safeway Store for $115,000, spent $150,000 for remodeling, and leased it to a school for $60,000 a year. On the strength of the lease, he was able to "mortgage out" so that with no money of his own, he was left with a cash flow of $6,000 a year. That's equivalent to earning $200,000, paying $100,000 in taxes and investing the remaining $100,000 at 6 per cent. And isn't it much easier converting a Safeway Store into a school than earning $200,000 in one year?

OLD CAR BARNS LIVE AGAIN

Conversions can be small, as from a gasoline station to a flower shop, or they can be extensive. In Salt Lake City, Utah, what was once the home of its streetcar system, has been transformed into a nostalgic center of recreational and commercial activity. Its restoration theme is the transportation of customers into a world of "yesterday happening today."

The conversion developers bought the old car barns consisting of 270,000 square feet for $1,000,000. What followed was an adventure in preservation and restoration. First, they sandblasted the old barn brick to its original vintage red. They had been covered for years with a thick layer of yellow paint. New floors were poured to cover old tracks. Overhead power lines were replaced with underground installations. Shrubs, grass, and flowers, landscaped to perfection, transformed the old slovenliness into tree-shaded brick plazas and fountain-adorned courtyards.

So much for beautification. Now comes the economic underpinning which pays for all this. Four movie theaters are now playing to enthusiastic audiences where the old 20,000 square foot machine shop used to be. The owners leased 8,000 square feet to what they claim is the largest old-fashioned ice cream parlor in the world. But that's just the beginning. By the time they finished, they gave Trolley Square, as it's called, the most interesting mix of tenants—a self-service gas station, a savings-and-loan office, farmers' market, open-air fair, bakery, fish market, fresh fruit and vegetable stands, several distinctive gift shops, health food store, leather outlet, wood carving and candle shop. And should you want to use this information as a springboard for what you may have in mind, here are a few more establishments where the old barns used to be; several restaurants, bookstore, greeting cards, jewelry store, pet shop, beauty parlor, optical office, flower garden, and a branch of the First Security Bank.

Here's private, urban renewal at its finest. Nothing is razed—everything is shored up, restored and preserved. Besides the immense contribution of revitalizing an old area, the entrepreneurs now have a real estate project that's going to provide them with substantial yearly incomes for many years. Here's another example of how everyone gains when creative people with feasible ideas brainstorm buildings and cause economic miracles to spring forth.

MY PERSONAL COMMITMENT TO CONSERVATION BRINGS UNDREAMED OF FINANCIAL REWARDS

I don't know whether my strong feelings for conservation came first and success second, or my success in shoring up old properties first, and concern for conservation second. But whatever the sequence, the results have been beyond my wildest dreams.

It all started when I bought a duplex and a coach-house garage at the rear of the lot. I knew nothing about real estate then, but it seemed logical to spend several hundred dollars to convert the garage into a cottage. I did, and quickly found a tenant to occupy it. I bought the duplex and coach house for $2,800 and sold them for $4,500. Converting the coach garage into living quarters brought a profit of $1,300.

I then bought a huge four-family for $4,000 in a shoddy neighborhood. The price was low because it was vacant most of the time. And no wonder! Each flat had eight cavernous rooms that looked more like a subdivided dirty barn than a home. But that didn't daunt me. I spent $4,000 remodeling it into 12 small, but spankingly clean apartments and filled them immediately with grateful tenants. I sold it for $12,000 and the buyer got a bargain. All this happened in the late 1930's.

After the war, I moved into bigger endeavors. I bought a seven unit apartment building for $35,000 with nine rooms in each flat and converted it into 40 small apartments at a cost of $35,000. The G.I.'s were grateful and I prospered. My rent roll was $30,000 a year. I subsequently used my $150,000 equity in this building to build the $3,000,000 Bockl Building ten years later.

I then tackled a commercial project. The five story, 50,000 square foot grocery building was a mecca for farmers 75 years ago.

They came from miles around at the turn of the century to sell their produce in town and stock up on groceries when they drove back to their farms. The hitching posts for their horses were still there—vintage Gay Nineties. After 75 years the building still smelled of coffee grindings. I bought it for $125,000, spent $75,000 for remodeling and filled it with printers, photographers, and commercial artists. I built up a rental of $75,000 a year and sold it for $260,000. After 25 years, it's still making money for the owner. The profit motive and conservation are natural partners. Each helps the other.

An elderly business executive owned an 80,000 square foot automobile garage building in an 80 per cent location which he half-heartedly converted into second- and third-rate office space. But the building was more than half vacant. The $40,000 gross rental barely covered his fixed expenses.

"Lease the building to me for 50 years with nothing down," I said, "and I'll pay you $20,000 a year."

"Why should I?" he asked.

"Because instead of losing $5,000 a year, you'll be making $20,000 a year, that's why."

After a week of negotiating, he saw the logic of my offer and accepted it.

I spent $75,000 remodeling it and leased the remaining space. I increased the rent from $40,000 to $90,000 a year and then sold my leasehold interest for $150,000. It was a deal that made everyone happy. The elderly owner was getting $20,000 a year instead of losing $5,000, blight was arrested, I earned $75,000 and the present owner is still netting $40,000 a year. The profit incentive and conservation made mutual contributions.

The quintessence—the high point of my conservation career—was remodeling a warehouse into a medical office building. I bought an empty 100,000 square foot, dust-laden, windowless building for $200,000. Its chief asset was location—a block from a hospital. How I financed and filled this "impossible dream" is a real estate saga which I detail in, *How Real Estate Fortunes Are Made,* pages 214 and 215.

These are a few of the buildings I've resuscitated and given new uses. Recycling buildings imaginatively is lucrative as well as challenging. It's a short cut to wealth. It digs down to the deepest roots of your financial, architectural, and aesthetic ingenuity. It's earning money at the highest conservational level.

TEN POINTS TO CHECK
BEFORE PLUNGING INTO THE CONVERSION
OF OLD PROPERTIES TO NEW USES

1. *Does the old architecture have character?* If it does you gain two ways. It adds interest to your conversion and saves money. Stained glass, old fireplaces, decorative plaster, aged wood beams, weatherbeaten clapboards, 60-year-old brick—all these linked functionally and imaginatively with modern additions add charm and help make the project financially feasible.

2. *Does the new use fit the old location?* Will a travel agency go where a gasoline station used to be? Or a mini-shopping mall where old buildings abound? Before you convert to a new use, be sure there is a need for it. How do you determine that? Get a demographic study from your local newspaper, analyze the character of the people in the immediate area, check road accessibility and then use your "sixth" sense before you plunge into your conversion project. Remember, you're plowing new ground and you have to dig deeper.

3. *Don't pour in a lot of money into a building that is on its last legs.* If the skeleton of the structure is not sound, it's not worth converting. As a rule, a steel and concrete building is a safer bet than a wooden structure, especially if its foundation has deteriorated. However, some wooden structures have a lot of life left and should not be thoughtlessly discarded.

4. *Conversions are tricky.* It's exceedingly difficult to gauge their cost. I've had several experiences where I misjudged by 50 to 100 per cent. One way to protect yourself against cost overruns is to buy the building to be converted at such a low price that even if your costs skyrocket you still have a chance to come out.

5. *Don't spend a lot of money changing a building into a fad use.* In Santa Barbara, California, I visited a discount store which was converted into a mini-mall of some 30 shops. There were no partitions between shops—everything was in the open. The owner probably didn't spend more than $100,000 to convert it. He was getting eight dollars a square foot for open space, and I'm sure he was making a lot of money. But for how long? Somehow the bazaar-like atmosphere

didn't appeal to me. I could feel its temporariness. Most of the shop owners had short term leases. Of course, I could be wrong. The open department store atmosphere, instead of individually partitioned shops, could be a fad that will last. I could see that the owner used good sense. He didn't spend a lot of money. Two good years and he's in the clear. That's the prudence I'd like you to use too.

6. *Getting financing for conversions is difficult.* It is easier to borrow on new construction. It's much easier to project costs and an operating statement on a new project than, let's say, converting an automobile garage building into a mini shopping mall. You might as well make up your mind to use your own money, or borrow whatever you need on your personal signature. Only when you've leased your conversion 80 per cent can you confidently go to a lender and ask for a permanent loan.

It's not a good way to finance, but in most cases, it's the only way. If you don't have a lot of cash, or can't show a solid financial statement, conversions are not for you. They're unpredictable, and lenders are more comfortable with things they can predict.

7. *Decide on a realistic rate per square foot.* Figure the rate for new use space before launching on a conversion. Before I decided on converting my automobile garage building into a mini-mall, I checked with a dozen retailers about what they could afford to pay. Rates could vary from three to eight dollars a square foot, depending on location and how much remodeling the tenant has to do. Do the same when converting a loft building into office space or low priced apartments. It's difficult to ascertain conversion costs; it should be easier to project income. At any rate, nail down as many variables as you can so you can get as close to the bottom line of the deal as possible.

8. *Don't get into a big conversion, especially the first time.* Since the variables are so elusive, the bigger the deal the more chance for error. Start off with changing a vacant gasoline station into an insurance office, for instance, but don't try converting a 300,000 square foot vacant brewery into a mall, offices or apartments.

9. *Tackle the big ones later.* When you have several successful conversions under your belt, or if you can get financial city backing, as some entrepreneurs did in Seattle, Washington, in a restoration pro-

ject known as Pioneer Square, then you can tackle the big ones. But not until then.

10. *Get a pre-construction lease commitment.* Just as a regional shopping center gets its start and financing when it obtains a pre-construction lease commitment from a major department store, so is it important that you get an anchor tenant for a mini-mall conversion. A well-financed theater operation or several successful restaurants will do. Then the little shops can live off their traffic. And vice versa, the interesting shops become magnets for people who will then become restaurant and theater patrons.

9

Chips of Real Estate Wisdom From My Files

A Certified Property Manager is a title given to anyone passing an examination dealing with technical and non-technical aspects of property management. It's not an easy examination, and those who pass it are regarded as experts in their field. But some of the most astute property managers I've known have never heard of a Certified Property Manager's degree. They developed their insights on the firing line of action.

MONEY-MAKING MANAGEMENT SECRETS

A friend of mine in Portland, Oregon, owns several small hotels. He's a director of the National Hotel Owners Association, not because of the size of his holdings, but because of his unusual management savvy.

"Smart management," he told me over a cool glass of lemonade on a warm day in Palm Springs, "consists of constantly paying attention to two things—upping income and lowering expenses. To increase income, you must know what people like and find unusual ways to tell it. To cut expenses you must use unorthodox methods without cutting down services."

"Let's take one at a time. What do people like and how do you tell it?"

"Courtesy, cleanliness and fair prices—that's what people like, in that order."

"And how do you tell it?"

"In addition to billboards, local magazines, and newspaper advertising, I give interesting gifts to gas station owners to direct lookers to my hotel, and I've distributed hundreds of boxes of candy to hotel clerks of competing hotels to send their overflow guests to me. I, in turn, send my overflow to them. Believe it or not, these two little ideas kick up my hotel revenue about $50,000 a year."

"And what unusual ideas do you have to keep expenses down?"

"I've got some dandies. Recently I was ordered to install a sprinkler system in an auditorium, and $8,000 was the lowest of several bids. I wasn't satisfied. I called a retired plumber who lived in a small town 50 miles away and said, 'Joe, how would you like a working vacation?' I described the job to him. 'Can I bring my wife too?' 'Sure,' I said. He bought the materials and within two weeks the job was completed. Cost: $3,700 and a free room and meals for two. I saved about $4,000 and put a little happiness in a retired couple's life."

"Any other ideas?"

"Well, since that happy cost-cutting incident, I've located and used a carpenter and a steam fitter the same way and saved thousands of dollars. But the best idea while somewhat philosophical is very practical. In observing people at work over the last 30 years, I've noticed three kinds—people who hate work, people who are indifferent to work and people who love work. I'm of the latter, so I recognize one when I see one.

"They're rare, and you must work hard to find them. And when you do, you've made a cost-cutting move right then and there. I practically have to force my three hotel managers to take vacations, or to cut down on their 70-hour weeks. They just love to work, they tell me. And I've staffed my hotel with hardworking people all down the line. The result? We're by far the most successful small hotel operators in the state, maybe in the country. My people are well paid, and my earnings year after year, are in the six figures."

MY FRIEND YOSSEL—HIS BUILDING SECRETS
MADE MILLIONS

With less than a third grade formal education, but with a Ph.D. in native ability, my friend Yossel developed three community shopping centers worth about $12,000,000. Each started with a few stores and grew as he got new tenants and made additions. There's nothing unusual about that, but what is unusual, is how he saved hundreds of thousands of dollars as he made these additions.

One of the tenants was a national movie theater company. They presented Yossel with a plan that called for definite specifications and a rental of $30,000-a-year minimum against a percentage of the gross. They knew from experience across the country that the building they wanted would cost about $300,000, including land, and were willing to pay $30,000 a year against percentage so that the lessor would realize a minimum of 10 per cent return. But our Yossel got a 20 per cent return because he built it for $150,000 including land. How? Let him tell it.

"I love looking for bargains! And when you're crazy about them, you find them. For instance, by carefully following the classified ads, I've been able to buy, and store for later use, electric fixtures, doors, paint, wallpaper, air conditioning units, carpeting, yes, even cement blocks. I usually buy these items for one-third the regular price. I then hire retired buddies of mine who were great mechanics in their day. While they work, I kibbitz, and they love it. I do this with brick layers, carpenters, electricians, carpet layers—you name it. For instance, that theater at my southside shopping center that normally costs $300,000 to build, I put up for $150,000. And since the land was there anyway, I'm netting a 20 per cent return. That's the way I built $12,000,000 worth of shopping centers. Good construction, good rents and good profits. You make a lot more money that way than calling a contractor and saying, 'Build it.' "

"But doesn't this kind of doing it all yourself leave no time for play?"

"I play golf six afternoons a week. I hold an eight handicap."

"What does that mean?"

"It means I shoot in the low eighties. Ten strokes better than my son and son-in-law, who are half my age."

"By the way, how old are you?"

"Over 65, and that's as close as I'll tell you."

"How do you manage to do all you're doing at your age?"

"Want to know the real secret?"

"Yes."

"I'm having a ball—I love to play and I love to work. I don't own the shopping centers any more. I turned them over to my children and grandchildren. I work for them. And you know something, I'm enjoying myself more making money for them, than they do spending it. But now I'm getting philosophical and that's not what you want."

"Oh yes, I do. Tell me, since you've made more money than all your educated children combined, what advice would you give to a young man getting started in real estate today?"

"Here it is in one sentence. Get as excited about sinking a ten-foot putt as about making a $10,000 deal. And never let go of this enthusiasm until you draw your last breath."

That's my friend Yossel, and he lives to the hilt.

THE TURTLE AND THE HARE—
A PHILOSOPHICAL FINANCIAL COMPARISON

This is a story of a race between one who played the stock market (the hare) and one who invested in real estate (the turtle). One was glib, quick, and restless; the other slow, plodding, and relaxed.

Dick, the slow one, averaged about $20,000 a year selling real estate. He lived frugally and began investing his savings early in his career using the leverage principle. He mortgaged out on a four-family here, a small commercial building there, and as his cash flow grew, he kept adding to his investment portfolio, all the while holding on to his job. When he was 55 years old, he was worth about $300,000 and enjoyed a net yearly income of about $30,000. He lived leisurely, traveled extensively and enjoyed a quiet, middle-class life.

Jim, the fast one, worked in an administrative capacity, and earned about $25,000 a year. Like Dick, he invested in real estate, but at a faster pace. At 40, he owned a 100-family apartment project which, had he kept it, could have retired him for life in grand style. But that was too slow for him. He sold it and with its proceeds, started playing the stock market. He was unluckily lucky. By the early 1960's, he was worth three-quarters of a million—on paper. To speed up his earnings, he borrowed $500,000 and put that in the market too. By 1973, he wheeled and dealed his common stock equities to $1,500,000, but foolishly didn't pay off the $500,000 bank loan. He believed in pyramiding.

"You believe in leveraging, don't you?" he retorted when I advised caution. "Well, I'm only doing in the market what you preach in your real estate books."

"But you're playing with dynamite. You're at the mercy of variables completely outside your control. Like shooting dice. In real estate, you are at the controls. When economic conditions change, you tighten management, you sell off, you consolidate. You use all your abilities to avert danger. But it's much more difficult protecting yourself from the whims of the mercurial stock market. It's like quicksilver—now you have it—now you don't."

"Words, words," he shrugged me off with one of his laconic smiles.

By the end of 1974, his plummeted stock had a paper value of $400,000 and he owed the bank $500,000. His creditors threatened to sell him out. He sold his two homes for $125,000 to stave them off. But he wasn't able to stave off the mental agony. Several of his friends pitched in to keep him afloat. And then, the Dow Jones mercifully rose to 875 and gave him a $100,000 cushion—a little peace. Perhaps he may rise again, or bite the dust again. That's not the way to live—in the attic or basement. The best place is in the living room, where you're in control.

I have another gripe against Jim's "hare" philosophy. It's not only too risky, but it's a "bare" philosophy, if you'll pardon the rhyme. It doesn't contribute any value to society. It's parasitic—playing and parleying with others' creations. It's not wholesome yoyoing your life up and down the Dow Jones, and making a bible out of stock market reports. It debilitates the mind.

Jim has a first class mind. He could have made a success in a half-dozen fields—law, business, medicine, music—but the fast-money syndrome robbed him of creativity.

Making money without making a contribution isn't fulfilling enough; it's settling for half the fun. Aristotle said that man was made for action—playing the market is not what he meant.

TIMING—TUNING YOUR RISKS TO YOUR AGE

There's a time to be born and a time to die. A time to buy and a time to sell. A time to risk and a time to play it safe. A time to climb and a time to rest.

If you've been planting 10,000 trees a year for 35 years and you're now 70 years old, should you stop planting trees? Not if you want to link yourself to the future. Keep on planting, but cut down to 1,000 trees a year so you can begin enjoying other activities you've always liked and found little time to do.

Perhaps it's reading the Bible, attending lectures, fishing, or playing more golf that you've always wanted. If owning property stands in the way, sell it to a capable young man via the conduit method, and put him to work to preserve your equity. Transfer your management problems to younger shoulders. Stabilize your income at a somewhat lower level—it's a small price to pay for more freedom. With more leisure, you can still get into interesting deals, but on a smaller and selective basis. This is no time to plant 10,000 trees a year. This is a time to be prudent, not bold.

But when you're 30, the accent should be on boldness, within prudent limitations. Don't overreach your abilities. For instance, some people are only comfortable dealing in five figures, others in six figures, and a few in seven. Don't strain your nervous system with sleepless nights if you're not at ease with deals beyond $100,000. One of my friends told me that he broke out in a cold sweat when he added up his debts during one of his quiet moments and found them to be $500,000. He began retrenching, even though he could have gotten into some excellent deals. I think he was wise, because pumping up a fortune at the price of pumping up his blood pressure wouldn't have made any sense. There's no point in flirting with coronary brinkmanship. It's better to live in peace with $20,000 a year than to live anxiously on the edge of a precipice earning $100,000 a year.

But for those between 30 and 40 who have strong nerves, a lot of natural ability, and a willingness to take on responsibility, I say borrow prudently as much as you can—and then coast while your properties are paying off the mortgages. By the time you're 60 to 65 you should be in an extremely safe equity position. Then convert it to an annuity by turning some, most or all of your properties to an upcoming young entrepreneur who will take on the responsibilities you did 25 years earlier. Then you can either continue making deals on a selective basis, or pursue your hobbies while the young man guards your interests with his energy, self-interest, and managerial skill. That's what the conduit method is all about, and that's why the timing of buying and selling is so crucially important.

The time to buy real estate to ripen 25 years hence, is when you're in the thirties. When you're 60 and over, you should be ripe with wisdom—the wisdom not to take long-shot chances—not if you enjoy the luxury of a stable income and need only to become involved in interesting projects where there are small or no risks. This is a time to relax, to remain free of any financial worries whatsoever. It's a time to stop champing at the bit, or getting into big deals just because you have more know-how now than you did 30 years ago. Keep busy, but not at the risk of invading your security. Spend time helping others, get into sure deals if you must, but without any personal liability to endanger what you've worked so hard to accumulate. Stay active, but be wise—tune your activity to your age.

A 62-year-old friend of mine who is worth $20,000,000 is in the midst of building $250,000,000 worth of properties for the government. Half of his working time, he's in the skies, flying to Hawaii, Alaska, Nevada, Arkansas, often crisscrossing the United States several times a week. He's making a mammoth contribution to our country, but is he fair to his family or himself? Even open-heart surgery a few years ago hasn't stopped him. But he's the exception, the unusual man who doesn't pay attention to timing. He's too involved, unwilling to get off the treadmill. It's understandable. He's mesmerized by the ease of making millions—and he won't or can't let go.

But would you take a job picking up and keeping 20-dollar bills for 15 years—providing you had to do it eight hours a day, six days a week? You'd be foolish if you did!

HOW A FOOLISH LANDLORD OUTSMARTED HIMSELF

More religion and irreligion is practiced in the heat of real estate action than in the cool, cloistered churches and synagogues. There are businessmen who use bluff and counter bluff, subtle cunning and backslapping diplomacy, but there are also those who stick to absolute honesty even if in the short run it costs them a lot of money. The latter are not only practicing genuine religion, but good business principles as well, because while the irreligious finaglers may get ahead in the short run, they invariably trick themselves behind the eight ball in the long run.

With this as a prologue, let me tell you a story of how bluffing collided with honesty, and lost.

Ray started a chain of restaurants that took off like gang busters. Ordinary location buildings that Ray leased turned into extraordinary money makers because he paid the owners 5 per cent against sale volume, and the rental was usually double what a normal fixed rent would have been.

One of the lessors built a $100,000 building on a $50,000 piece of land and leased it to Ray for 5 per cent for ten years with a ten year option. He averaged about $30,000 a year rent during the prime lease, and when Ray was ready to renew the option for another ten years, he said to the owner:

"We've made money in your building and so did you. It was mutually profitable, and I'm happy for both of us. But before renewing the lease, I'd like you to freshen up the building a little."

"How much do you have in mind?" the owner asked brusquely.

"Oh, about $10,000," Ray replied.

"Nothing doing. You're probably making $75,000 a year on my property so what's $10,000. Spend it yourself."

"But if you don't, I may not renew the lease."

"You'd have to be crazy not to renew a money maker like you've got in my building."

"I may just be that crazy. Think it over. Let me know in a week."

"The answer is emphatically no. I don't have to think it over."

"All right, have it your way," and Ray left.

Several blocks away there was a lot for sale. Ray bought it for $75,000. Several weeks later he sent an official notice that he was not renewing the lease.

The owner called Ray the next day: "Look, if you're really serious about moving, hell, I'll spend the $10,000."

"You're too late. I'm building a new restaurant two blocks away."

"But you've got a good one in my building. Why spend the money?"

"I would've stayed if you had acted like a gentleman. But you tried to bluff me, and I decided to call your bluff."

The owner tried to cajole and sweet talk Ray into a receptive mood.

"I'll spend $20,000 if you stay," he said in desperation.

"The answer is still no."

Ray built his restaurant a short distance away and started doing business at the rate of $700,000 a year. His former landlord's building was vacant for a year. In desperation he rented it to a third-rate operator at a third the rent he was getting, and even that ended soon. Between vacancies and low rentals the foolish landlord has lost over $100,000 during the last several years; all because he tried to use cunning instead of honesty.

GOING FIRST CLASS SOUNDS GOOD
BUT MAY THROW YOU INTO FINANCIAL STEERAGE

Going first class is an attractive idea, but it can get you into all sorts of trouble—as happened to my friend and associate (discussed in Chapter 4) when he built four first class motels in four small towns and began losing money in each the moment he opened. Few enjoyed his first class amenities because few could afford them. In contrast to the "going first class" syndrome, another friend of mine, Ben, who had x-ray business vision, built a 100-room motel in a small town for $7,500 a room, and pricing it at $9.50 a night, enjoyed 75 per cent occupancy the first month, and increased it to 80 per cent before he finished the year. He netted $60,000 the first year. I asked him how he did it after telling him about my friend's failures with the four motels.

"Your friend served his pride. I serve the needs of people—what they can afford. You don't build a luxury skyscraper in Sheboygan because it was successful in Chicago or New York.

"Before I built my 100-room motel, I did a lot of thinking. Who sleeps in small-town motels? I found out. They're not executives on expense accounts. They are people several rungs down the ladder who hack out a living by keeping a watchful eye on expenses. They gladly give up frills for savings. They travel lightly and spend lightly.

"With this austere thinking, I called in several architects and challenged them to design a bare, functional room and bath, 12 x 22, for $5,500. I told them I'd get the land for $1,000 a room and furnish it for $1,000 a room. 'I want a key job,' I said, '100 rooms, completely furnished for $750,000.'

"They tried and couldn't do it. Then one enterprising man said, 'I'll do it if you can get a small contractor to bid 10 per cent below the usual pricing.' I approached a father and son carpenter team and offered them this and other small hotel jobs, if they worked exclusively for me, and could deliver at $5,500 a room. They agreed, and we're now building our third motel."

"Why did you pick the 100-room size motel?"

"Because a mamma-papa team can take care of 100 rooms as easily as the 40 rooms your friend built. Cutting expenses and passing them on to users, is the key to success in these budget motels. It took a lot of work to produce a clean, comfortable room for $9 a night, and we're reaping the rewards. The guests are delighted and so am I. By the time you write your next book, we'll probably have several dozen of these 'budgettells' operating in the Middle West. Budgettells—hey, that's a good name for a chain."

HOW TO PREPARE FOR THE BUYING END OF THE CONDUIT TECHNIQUE

Develop an interest in property management. Talk to successful managers, ask questions, get their insights. Read books on real estate management, take night courses and eventually take the C.P.M. examination to become a Certified Property Manager. Then get into a few small deals: duplexes, four families, eight families—to get the feel of what you've learned.

If you think you're ready to step into a bigger project, like a $250,000 to $500,000 office building, a small apartment building project or shopping center, then compile a list of people over 60 who own such real estate, and telephone one after the other in this manner:

"Mr. Harris (or whatever his name), could you please spare 30 minutes? I'd like to meet you and explain an idea I have for your property (state address), that may interest you."

If he says his property is not for sale, then counter with, "I'm not exactly suggesting a conventional sale, but an idea to convert your property into a trouble-free annuity." Of 20 calls, I'll wager 10 will say:

"Well, there's no harm in talking. Come over."

Tell each that you've read a book by George Bockl, in which he explains an interesting theory called the conduit technique where both seller and buyer gain in the sale of property. Then proceed to tell its advantages. Practice the presentation at home until it becomes crystal clear in your mind before you attempt to explain it. A lot of money hangs in the balance.

Some will show no interest, and others, especially if they're tired of management, will ask you to go into it in more detail. It might not be a bad idea to send each potential seller a paperback copy of my book, calling his or her attention to the chapters that deal with the conduit technique.

If you make 20 presentations, I assure you, you're bound to get several interesting responses. Assess each one, pick out the most congenial owner, the best property, the best terms and consummate a deal. You and the seller will be the gainers, and I will receive my reward in knowing that somewhere out there my efforts have done some good.

A FEW THOUGHTS ABOUT THE RELATIONSHIP
BETWEEN INTEREST RATES AND PRICE

With the advent of two-digit interest rates, the value of real estate took a nosedive in spite of inflation. The reason is simple—third party financing with 10 per cent interest drastically reduces the net income of property. And since the net income approach is the most used method in determining the value of investment real estate, the high interest rate cuts a big chunk out of its price. The fact that it would cost more money to reproduce the real estate does not alter the equation when 10 per cent interest has to be plugged in as a yearly fixed expense.

For instance, if a buyer has to pay $10,000 a year interest on a $100,000 loan instead of $6,000 as was the case a few years ago, and rents can be raised to pick up only $2,000 of the differential, then theoretically and practically, the property has dropped about $20,000 in value.

If a four-family costing $100,000 to reproduce shows only a $6,500 net because of high interest rates, then its value must be realistically pegged to $65,000, based on an expected 10 per cent return, or $54,160 if the buyer insists on a 12 per cent return.

When the interest rate was 6 per cent, the capitalization rate was 8 per cent, usually 2 per cent above the current interest rate. Therefore, when a property had a net profit of $8,000 before debt service, it's valuation was arrived at by dividing $8,000 by 8 per cent or $100,000. But when interest is 10 per cent, and the expected capitalization rate is 12 per cent, a property yielding $8,000 is now valued on the basis of $8,000 divided by 12 per cent, or $66,666.

Now what happens when you confront an elderly owner in a conduit situation who has been used to an 8 per cent capitalization rate to value his property?

If you tell him his property on a cash basis is worth only two-thirds of what is was worth several years ago when the capitalization rate was 8 per cent, he'll feel offended, and won't even listen to your logical explanation that when current interest rate is 10 per cent, the capitalization rate ought to be 12 per cent because there's added risk in owning property. You'll have to come up with a wiser approach. Let him have the higher price, but compensate it by suggesting a sale on a land contract with a long amortization and a lower interest rate, say 6 per cent.

For instance, if his property is worth only $650,000 on the basis of third party 10 per cent mortgage, offer him $1,000,000 if he'll finance it for you at 6 per cent. Remember, this is how the shopping center was sold to the young auto mechanic described in Chapter 3. The owner will squirm a little at the 6 per cent when the going rate is 10 per cent, but the high $1,000,000 price should tend to relax him. Another good argument to use, if he's still hesitant, is to suggest that if he insists on a higher interest rate, there would be little or no cash flow left. Such a situation would make it a poor deal for both buyer and seller—for buyer, with no cushioning cash flow the deal would become shaky; for seller, it would jeopardize his continuing stream of income. Emphasize the truism that what's a good deal for each, is the best deal for both.

Don't let high interest rates stop you from making deals. The equalizing factor of raising the price and lowering the interest rate often makes an impossible deal possible.

DON'T TRY TO CONDOMINIUMIZE AN OFFICE BUILDING

One day, an advertising executive came to my office and announced excitedly:

"George, you're always looking for new ideas. I've got one that's a pip."

"What is it?"

"You know how the condominium idea has swept the housing industry. Well, I've met a guy who's going to condominiumize an office building. That could sweep the country too. You ought to get in on it."

"I'm sorry to dampen your enthusiasm, but I don't think it's such a great idea. In fact, it's a bad one. You notice, it's not sweeping anything."

"Why?"

"For these reasons: Let's say you condominiumize a doctors' medical building of 30,000 square feet. You'd probably have to deal separately with about 40 doctors—a tremendously difficult task. Assuming you've hurdled the selling job, here are some problems that could come up in the future. What if one of the doctors buys 700 square feet, and three years later, wants to take in a partner who needs another 500 square feet? He's stuck, if he's locked in on both sides with doctors who need no changes. But if he's renting, he has maneuverability—he can either get larger space in the same building, or move to another."

"Yeh, I see the problem," my friend said, his enthusiasm waning. "But what about the advantages—pride of ownership and the tax gain because of depreciation?"

"They're not enough to counter the big disadvantages. And here's another. How would you like to practice in a building with 40 bosses? It's one of those ideas that looks good on paper, but won't work in practice."

"Well, I tried."

"Try again. The next one may be a good one."

HOW TO DEAL WITH UNREASONABLE AND ECCENTRIC TENANTS

On a New Year's Day, while I was vacationing in Palm Springs, I received a call from Los Angeles, which happened to be the headquarters of a multi-state company that was using 7,000 square feet of office space in my building in Milwaukee. The president was on the phone:

"Your ineptitude cost me $1,000, and by golly, you're going to pay for it." he snarled angrily.

"What did I do?"

"There's no heat in your Milwaukee office building. I've arranged a telephone conference between my Los Angeles attorney and accountant to discuss important matters with my attorney and accountant in Milwaukee. It was so cold in your building we had to call it off. It cost me $1,000 to arrange this conference and you're paying for it."

How does one react to an unexpected outburst like this? These things immediately flashed through my mind. He was paying $25,000 a year rental and his lease was up for renewal in April. I knew that whatever caused the heat loss would not interest him. Trying to rationalize the heat loss would only infuriate him. Yet, do I agree to a $1,000 loss just like that?

"I'll check it and call you back," I said, stalling for time. I didn't want to agree or disagree.

"You can check it all you want. I'm deducting $1,000 from the next month's rent." And he hung up.

I called my office and found that the Merchant Police who were supposed to check the boiler every two hours on holidays, either didn't catch it or failed to make the rounds. Six hours after the scheduled telephone conference, the building was as warm as a fur hat. But it was too late. The damage was done.

The next day I dictated a letter to my Milwaukee secretary over the phone which went something like this:

Dear Ken:
Whether you were damaged $1,000 worth or not
is not the point. You were inconvenienced—

that's the main point. Your goodwill is worth
more to me than $1,000, therefore deduct it from
the rent. I will promptly alert my management so
it doesn't happen again."
Cordially,
George

I received a curt: "Thank you for your understanding and
goodwill."

In April, we renewed our lease for another three years at a higher
rental. The negotiations were friendly and pleasant. Had I self-
righteously tried to rationalize myself out of the $1,000, I'm sure I'd
have jeopardized the new $90,000 three-year lease. I don't think I
yielded on any point of principle. I simply took an overall pragmatic
view and under the circumstances, made a good decision.

WHEN CORNERED IN A BAD DEAL,
THE SOONER YOU TAKE THE LOSS, THE BETTER

About five years ago, a wealthy real estate bargain hunter
bought what in the 1920's was the most prestigious 1,000 room hotel
in our town. He got it at the breathtakingly low price of $5,000,000,
with a $500,000 cash down payment and a $4,500,000 mortgage. He
spent about $500,000 rejuvenating the public areas to attract the
lucrative convention business. "All I need," he told me, "is 50 per
cent occupancy and I'm in the black."

But he didn't get 50 per cent occupancy and he lost $500,000 the
first year. Halfway into the second year, he was still showing heavy
losses. He got panicky and did something about it. He called in one of
the large hotel chains of America and began negotiating for the sale of
his "bargain." He told them he wasn't a top-notch operator, and that
perhaps with their national expertise, they could do what he couldn't.
He offered to sell the hotel subject to the outstanding $4,500,000
mortgage. It would mean, he told them, a loss of $500,000 in equity
money and $500,000 in improvements—a total $1,000,000 loss.

That certainly seemed like an offer they couldn't refuse. But they
did.

"And you know," my friend told me during a round of golf, "I
had to fork over an additional $500,000 in cash before they were

willing to assume the $4,500,000 mortgage. I did, and it was the smartest move of my career."

The national experts, preceded by a flurry of $1,000,000 worth of renovation and promotion, took over the hotel, installed their time-tested operational systems and gave it their multi-million dollar image. But it was not enough to revive the dying 1,000-room hotel. After a year of revved up operations, the national chain owners must still have shown a huge loss because they approached a wealthy friend of mine to buy their hotel.

"I'll buy," my friend told them, "but at a loser's price."

"Like what?"

"Like paying me $1,300,000 in cash to assume your outstanding $4,500,000 mortgage."

After several months of negotiations, my friend got his $1,300,000 in cash and the hotel subject to the outstanding mortgage. What happened next was the reverse of what his predecessors did. He scrapped their major premise of retaining the 1,000 rooms and gutted the entire inside of the hotel. He used this line of reasoning:

At today's prices, it would cost $60,000 a room to build a modern 500-room hotel, complete with public areas and adequate parking. He would convert the 1,000 outdated rooms into 550 new ones, remodel the original four floors of public areas, build a modern parking structure—all for $7,000,000. By buying the hotel for $3,100,000, his total cost of a practically brand new 550-room hotel would be $10,000,000, or less than $20,000 a room. At a third of the cost of any modern hotel, he would be in a very favorable competitive position.

He was right. The hotel has been rebuilt close to within his budget, and it's a beauty. His four distinctive restaurants are beehives of activity, and the room occupancy is creeping up to where it's beginning to make money. Where other hotels are in a bind when their occupancy drops to 60 per cent, he feels comfortable even with 50 per cent because of his low cost per room and low debt service. And when his occupancy reaches 70 per cent as he says it will, his profit margin will zoom past that of new hotels which had to spend $60,000 instead of $20,000 a room.

I realize this story is not applicable to the average reader, but the principle that works in a $10,000,000 deal should also work in a $100,000 deal.

Knowing how to change the major premise of your thinking can work economic miracles. By converting 1,000 inadequate rooms into 550 modern ones, my friend built a $30,000,000 hotel for $10,000,000!

HOW TO DEVELOP THE SIXTH SENSE

First, what do we really mean by the sixth sense? Isn't it the encompassing with a single intuitional comprehension the bedrock common sense of a situation? But this intuitional comprehension does not come to anyone who has not toiled in overcoming obstacles, in solving problems. His hunch comes from a background of experience out of which he draws the right decisions. Without this input there's no output.

But why do some get this input quicker than others? Why are some wise at 35 and others fools at 70?

I'd like to answer these questions with another question. Why are some children mathematical geniuses at 10, or musical prodigies at 8? Is it just happenstance, blind, random, occurrences? I think not. If you'll permit a spiritual opinion, I'd like to suggest that we inherit talents from past lives. In other words, I subscribe to the theory of reincarnation as the most plausible explanation for the various attitudes and propensities people develop in their lifetimes. Environmental factors, of course, play a role, but the accumulated experiences of past lives, to which scientists refer as DNA or genetic information, play the main role.

How does all this relate to real estate? It gives me a cue why some men have this sixth sense and some don't. Why some look at a property and instantaneously grasp its essentials, while others look but see very little.

Several friends of mine have x-ray business vision. One of them looked at my oil-slicked automobile garage that I was remodeling into a mini-mall, and said, "Two small theaters ought to do well here." Then he proceeded without a moment's hesitation to zero in on the economics of the deal so it made sense to me, as the lessor, and to him, as the lessee.

Why didn't I think of it? He had more experience in solving theater problems than I. That's why his computerized mind spilled out the information almost instantaneously. He had a highly developed sixth sense.

And eventually you will too, if you do the following. When confronted with an array of new facts and situations, clear your mind of the usual chatter. Empty it so there's room for new thoughts to come in. But don't kid yourself, you won't be able to empty it while you're on the run, hurrying from one usual haunt to another. Get into a quiet place and have a quiet time. Relax...Meditate...Soothe your mind...Let your tensions slowly dissolve...Let go of all thoughts....

The new or transcending thoughts that will come into a quieted mind will give you more insights than if you try relaxing at a bar, football game, or watching "Kojak" on television. Transcending thoughts, whether you're interested in raising the quality of your life or getting a clearer perspective on a real estate deal, are the insights which prod and develop your sixth sense—the comprehensive wisdom.

Try to have a daily quiet time. It will reduce tensions and increase your energy. But more important, a fresh mind will give new guidance and purpose to your life. It might even quiet your mind so you'll "hear" God speak in terms of insights that will speed your journey Godward—far more important than making a good real estate deal.

10

How You Can Use Innovative Money-Making Ideas From Foreign Countries

A doctor visiting abroad looks for medical innovations, a businessman for new merchandising ideas. When I travel, I look for new real estate insights.

I learned a great deal in the foreign countries I visited. Here are some interesting and practical examples of how people in faraway lands solved their real estate problems in unusual ways.

HOW A SWISS TOUR GUIDE FINANCED A 50-ROOM RESORT BY BARTERING FUTURE VACATIONS FOR WORKERS' MOONLIGHTING HOURS

I met him in Geneva—a charming guide whose knowledge of Swiss history enlivened every city and valley we visited. But he did more than describe Switzerland; he gave me a real estate idea that is as innovative as it is practical.

Having been a travel guide for ten years, he knew what vacationers liked—beautiful countryside, cozy resorts (about 50 rooms), quaint architecture, unusual cuisine and personalized owner hospitality. He wanted to build such a resort, but he couldn't get the financing to build it.

But he had an idea. Why not trade future vacations for building money. Here's how he did it. He bartered $40,000 worth of future vacations for a five-acre piece of land at the foot of a mountain, overlooking a beautiful small lake. An architect drew the plans for 30 paid vacation days to be used during the next five years. The travel guide found plumbers, electricians, carpenters, painters, etc., who were willing to spend their weekends, evenings and holidays working on his resort in return for paid vacations in proportion to the number of hours they logged on his project.

It took two years of moonlighting hours to build the innovatively financed resort, and when the guide, now turned owner, opened for business, one-third of his guests were the "financiers," collecting their free vacations. However, the paying patrons more than met his fixed expenses since he had no debt service. He had a profit as soon as he opened.

Paying off a labor debt is a more primitive financial approach than our sophisticated piggy-back, wrap-around, floating-interest rates and sales-lease back innovations, but when the refined mortgage techniques are beyond the scope of the ordinary man, a basic approach can be refreshingly practical.

It takes an engaging personality and unusual salesmanship to put together a project the way this travel guide did. It's not for the ordinary person. But if you have a background of travel, a host's personality, a fervent desire to own a resort, but little money, then perhaps this unusual success story can give you a cue for solving your problem.

If it worked in Switzerland, it could work here—so don't give up too quickly if it sounds unbelievable.

HOW SWISS BUILDINGS AND VILLAGES CREATE CHARM, AND FUNCTION TO MAKE MONEY FOR THEIR OWNERS

The Swiss people are among the most resourceful in the world. They know how to milk the last drop of income from their properties. My wife and I stayed in a 150-year-old hotel in Lausanne and didn't mind paying $60 a day because it was so charmingly kept up. The wooden window sills were cracked and weather beaten, but they were freshly painted and embellished below with rows of bright red geraniums. The dining room ceiling was of domed glass, and the bright light that streamed in from above dappled the room with an open air hue. The vividly colored flower gardens that hugged the windows on three sides made us feel we were dining in a veritable fairyland.

The Swiss people defy our rules of obsolescence. We're supposed to write off a building in 50 years. Their buildings are just entering the prime of life at that age. That's because they have a reverence for maintaining property—one of the distinctive marks of a civilized society.

One of Switzerland's most charming and oldest villages is Gruyère. It's about the size of hundreds of small clusters of buildings that dot the countryside and take a minute or two to pass by automobile. But this one was about a block off the highway. We parked our car and joined the throngs of tourists who were walking up and down its single cobblestone street. The charmingly quaint buildings were like expensive, blown-up antiques—multi-colored, weather beaten—a harmonious blend of old stone, brick and wood—and flowers everywhere—in boxes along the second floor windows, inside the shops and along walkways between stores.

The villagers merchandised their charm with the expertise of Madison Avenue, and with the wisdom of the Swiss. When we stopped for lunch at one of the half-dozen small restaurants, we were as impressed with their sincere courtesy as we were with their 200-year-old architecture.

The delicious ham, fresh homemade bread, the variety of cheeses, the morning-picked loganberries in the richest cream I'd ever tasted, was a meal as unforgettable as the snowy mountain crags that etched indelibly on my mind.

Without Swiss resourcefulness, Gruyère could easily have slipped into poverty and obsolescence. There are a thousand such villages in America that have become drab and nondescript. But in their defense, Americans might say that we can't do what the Swiss do, because we don't have the tourists. But if the Swiss didn't do what they do, they wouldn't have the tourists either.

Swiss real estate ranks among their most valuable assets. Each home, office, factory and store produces many more times the return of equivalent American properties because the length of their use is many times longer than ours. If longevity is part of value, as it is, then it's understandable why their stock of buildings is worth perhaps five-fold the value of similar buildings in America.

This conserving Swiss attitude has carried over into industry and finance. It's no accident that their factories are as well run as their Swiss watches, and the Zurich money managers are among the most dependable in the world.

You can't make a good omelet out of bad eggs. Too many squandering people, grandstanding with ostentatious consumption, don't make a stable society. Sooner or later it dead-ends into shor tages and inflation. The habit of replacing our multi-billion dollar stock of real estate about every 50 years is a dangerous syndrome. It may raise our Gross National Product, but it will eventually drain our credit and resources.

If conservation is a mark of a civilized society, then we would do well to emulate the Swiss.

A EUROPEAN IDEA NOW FLOURISHING ON THE OUTSKIRTS OF MILWAUKEE

A German born advertising executive with a flair for the unusual decided to bring a bit of Europe to his city. He called it Stonecroft—named after Mr. Stone, the entrepreneur—a street of two-story structures with living quarters up and shops down—right in the middle of a 40-acre farm about 20 miles from Milwaukee.

It reminded me of Gruyère, Switzerland. An arched brick entrance led to a two block long street with joined multi-architectured houses on either side. Each 25-foot frontage was different—with French, German, Scandinavian and Swiss motifs dominating the interesting variety. But because it was new, it didn't have the charm of Gruyère. Like old wine and authentic antiques, it takes time for a town to acquire bouquet and character.

The people who bought these shops and living quarters were grateful for Stonecroft—it offered them a life style they could not otherwise experience.

A widow who bought one of the units showed me through her living quarters.

"Look at this view," she said. "Beautiful fields as far as the eye can reach. At night, I hear chirping crickets instead of noisy automobiles. And during the day, I'm in my bookstore downstairs, meeting interesting people who come to browse or buy. I earn enough from my business to make my mortgage payments and part of my living expenses. It's a wonderful life and I'm grateful to Mr. Stone for daring this development."

The same sentiment was expressed by the woodcarver, ship modeler, sandwich-shop proprietor, artist and others.

Mr. Stone's motive for developing this condominium concept was partly profit, but mostly a desire to reconstruct the nostalgic environment of his Teutonic boyhood days.

"A great deal of the old world serenity I had known, I'm sure, stemmed from the small European buildings and shops," Mr. Stone volunteered. "Small, human scale buildings sooth; big buildings and big stores excite. Stonecroft is an attempt to encourage quiet relationships."

"You've now sold 20 buildings," I said. "How many more?"

"Thirty at most. I want to keep it small and personal."

"Has it been profitable?"

"Only modestly, but it's been extremely profitable in another way."

"How?"

"I've made 20 families happy, including my own. I live upstairs in one of the buildings and have my art shop below. I have the best of two worlds—I've recaptured the tranquility I had known and I'm enjoying the opportunities and freedoms I find here."

As I was driving home after viewing Stonecroft, I was ruminating how developers had made billions centralizing real estate and people into huge complexes, and now that congestion has been tried and found wanting, the pendulum is swinging back, and billions will be made decentralizing them. Trial and error is part of the civilizing process. We've erred in developing into ant-hill megalopolises, but people are beginning to see their mistakes and will revert to a human scale of living again. Innovators like Stone are pioneering a healthy social change from the alienation of skyscrapers and cavernous department stores to a more relaxed relationship between man and man, and between man and his shelter.

Wouldn't it make social sense to sprinkle our decaying downtowns with Stonecrofts? By recycling neglected structures and building small new ones, we could make a healthy, pervasive, horizontal impact on an area rather than build more skyscrapers on half-square blocks and let the surrounding properties decay. That's what happened in the past, and that's what we have now—tall buildings surrounded by blight.

Our downtowns are not going to be revitalized by a few more skyscrapers. They will, by dozens of Stonecrofts.

HOW A MAN IN JOHANNESBURG, SOUTH AFRICA, TURNED MINERS' HUTS INTO APARTMENTS

About a year ago, I received a letter from one of the largest property management firms in Johannesburg, South Africa. It read:

> Dear Mr. Bockl:
>
> "We want to thank you for writing, *How Real Estate Fortunes Are Made.* It gave us some new and practical ideas on real estate development which we had not thought of in our country. We plan to put them into practice."
>
> I replied:
>
> "I'm glad to share my country's knowledge with you. In fact, I'm flattered that people so far away would be interested in what we do here. But now, you can do us a favor. I'm preparing material for another book. Would you share some unusual Johannesburg real estate insights which we can apply in America?"
>
> Within a week, the Johannesburg Realtor replied:
>
> "Thank you for your letter of February 17, 1975. You will observe that I have been appointed a Director of this company, which is the largest property management firm in the country. We administer about 700 buildings and nearly 20,000 individual tenants.

"In reply to your request for an unusual South African deal, I have one which must rank as a coup by any standards anywhere.

"On the outskirts of Johannesburg in a rundown residential area, is "Villa Barcelona," some photographs of which are enclosed. Many years ago, this was an ugly barracks, looking like a prison or a fort, which accommodated gold miners from the countryside and surrounding African States. It was the most grim looking place imaginable and accommodated a few thousand men in cold, uninviting primitive conditions. Over the years, the mine closed down leaving the eyesore which was slowly encroached on by sub-economic houses.

"No one knew what to do with the monster until a local property man bought it for ground value, about a million dollars, and proceeded to transform it into a Spanish-type apartment building of some 250 flats. Each flat is modern and delightful. There are tennis courts, shops, and amenities of every kind within the enormous square.

"The cost of refurbishing was in the region of one million dollars and the present value is of the order of two and a half million, and probably more. I consider the project a perfect example of finding higher and better use for an apparently valueless structure.

"Now I am stumped in my efforts to find a better use for a building I am working on as per the enclosed photographs taken on a Sunday from the freeway. "Grosvenor" is a large Ford Agency occupying a vast motor showroom and workshop. The building covers 90,000 square feet and the floor area is nearly 300,000 square feet. The owner values the building at four million rand (about 5 million dollars) and theoretically, the value is there. The area and building is far too valuable to be used as a motor workshop and motor dealers in our city are generally moving to the suburbs.

"The heavy concrete pillars rule out a cinema complex. It is just out of the C.B.D. (central business district) shopping and office area by about three blocks. The intersection is about the busiest bottleneck during the week. The larger department stores are not interested.

"I am working on an idea for a business called Wheels, a supermarket for cars or anything associated with wheels, e.g., car showrooms, motor cycles, spares, lawn mowers, bicycles, speedshops, caravans, motor homes, perhaps even boats, prams, toys, etc. In theory the idea is good but it is new and unproven.

"There's a challenge for you. Let's earn a nice commission together in Africa."

I wasn't interested in any commission, but I was intrigued with the challenge of Grosvenor Square.

I offered this suggestion:

"You indeed have a very interesting challenge in the Grosvenor Square building. Several ideas come to mind.

"I visited St. Thomas Island in the Caribbean several years ago where an innovative entrepreneur converted about 500,000 square feet of old buildings that pirates had used to store their booty several centuries ago, into a shopping center for small stores catering to tourists. The typical store was from 1,000 to 5,000 square feet, and varied in goods from jewelry, cameras, antiques, local crafts, china, and glassware, to tiny restaurants, rugs, linens, clothing stores, and art shops—a collage of goods featuring an international flavor. This is one idea for your Grosvenor.

"Here's another one. In our country, a man in San Francisco converted a factory building of about 400,000 square feet into a similar project featuring a variety of stores. I would suggest a similar usage for Grosvenor, and if possible, set aside one floor for parking so that prospective customers could park and shop. I would think your space should bring about $5 a square foot a year. If that could be done, the building could theoretically generate over a million dollars a year in gross rent.

"I feel that your "Wheels" idea would be too limiting, whereas the shopping mall idea would open it to a greater variety of uses, and thus increase your chances of success.

"Thank you for your Villa Barcelona story. Good luck on your Grosvenor."

We both gained by this exchange of information. Sharing knowledge is more fun than hoarding or selling it to the highest bidder.

A REVOLUTIONARY IDEA CONVERTS FOUR FAILING BUILDINGS INTO A SUCCESSFUL MALL

Vacationing and working is a healthy mixture. One reinforces the other—work takes the boredom out of too much leisure, and some leisure softens the intensity of work.

It was with this thought that I left for a ten-day research trip through western Canada, hoping to find some new ideas for my readers. I visited Calgary, Vancouver and Victoria, and on the way I treated myself to nature's wonders in the beautiful area of Banff, Lake Louise and Jasper.

Calgary was my first stop and I found a gem of an idea—Penny Lane Mall in the heart of downtown. I didn't dig into the financial aspects of this unusual project, but I think I can reconstruct the deal from what I've seen.

The entrepreneur, whoever he is, was an enterprising individual. He combined five adjoining 75-year-old buildings into a three-story mall. What were five old basements, five third-rate first floor stores and five second floor vacant areas, were imaginatively converted into about 40 stores. The combined area of the five old buildings was about 100 by 250, so that the three floors yielded about 75,000 square feet. Subtracting 20 per cent for washrooms, stairwells and three center lanes, left about 60,000 square feet of net rentable area.

Assuming the rent at $5.00 a square foot net to owner, the income would be about $300,000 a year. Let's suppose the enterpriser paid $500,000 for the five old buildings and spent $1,000,000 converting them, he would then have a 20 per cent return investment. A big return, but he is entitled to it because he took a big risk.

As I went through the varied and attractively built shops, I did some thinking. Why did the entrepreneurs of 75 years ago build five stores with all the wasted space in the basements and upper levels? Why did they plan outside entrances so that customers had to bear the cold going from one store to another? And oh, does it get cold in Calgary!

How logical it is to have 40 small stores rather than five big stores, and how much more sense it makes to shop in a comfortable climate-controlled mall than going in and out in mid-winter from a cold street into a hot store. Why didn't people think of these advantages 75 years ago?

As I asked these questions, I slowly began to get my answers. Why didn't we get electricity 200 years ago? Or the telephone? It takes time. So many wise answers are still wrapped up in the wonderful law of evolution.

Who knows what's still beyond the mall idea. And for that matter, who knows what dazzling plans are still ahead for our lives. Faith in the constant betterment of whatever we're doing is what fuels our evolution and widens our vision.

A TALE OF TWO QUARRIES

On my way to Canada, I met a retired executive who told me how a real estate man in North Hollywood filled an empty quarry with dirt and made a fortune. The enterpriser's plan was as simple as it was logical. The owners of the exhausted quarry looked upon it as a big hole that had no further benefit. All the valuable lime was out of the ground, and they were ready to get rid of it. At the same time, a young entrepreneur was ready to get into it. He didn't see it as a hole in the ground, but as a dumping area to be filled with millions of truckloads of junk, refuse and dirt. He bought it dirt cheap (pardon the pun), and in three years filled it, getting hundreds of thousands of dollars from people who paid $1.25 a load to dump their refuse. That ended phase one of his money making operation.

Phase two found him filling the accumulated junk with good clean earth, and landscaping it into a beautiful industrial park site. The land happened to be in a good industrial area and he cleaned up another fortune selling it at a good price. It was an interesting story.

But not as interesting as the one I found in Victoria, Canada. There a Mrs. Robert Pine Butchart, sensitive to the bleakness of an abandoned lime quarry which her husband emptied in his manufacture of Portland cement, decided to landscape it because her home was close by.

Thus began a "gardening" experiment that was soon to have far reaching results. Through the skillful mixture of rare and exotic shrubs, trees and plants, often personally collected by Mr. and Mrs. Butchart during their extensive world travels, the now world-famous Butchart Gardens were created.

As I walked through the 30 acres of what once was an exhausted lime quarry, I shook my head in disbelief at the breath-taking beauty. The Garden of Eden could not have surpassed its splendor.

As I slowly walked under a clear late-August sky, my response to beauty was suffused by a collage of color, the fragrance of flowers and the varied arrangements of trees, shrubs and plants. It was an unreal and overpowering experience. I was transported into a paradise, transformed into a new man, transfixed by a beauty I had never known before.

The path begins with a rich green lawn and a limpid pool of sky-blue water. Then you lose yourself in arboreal splendor against a background of native dogwood on one side and rambling roses festooned on pillars on the other. Dwarf pink and blue viscaria edge the border of the walk. The border slopes away to a lawn which is dotted with exceptionally fine specimens of native maples.

After a half a block I came to a sign, "Up the Steps to the Sunken Gardens." I noticed that the handrails beside the steps were made of cement, fabricated to look like wood. I reached the top and looked down 50 feet below—an unbelievable panorama of color. The quarry walls were hung with ivy and Virginia creepers. Directly below was a path winding through a large rockery where gentians, saxifrages, lithospermum, Lebanon candytuft, pentstemons and other rock and alpine plants abound. At the bottom the path continued gracefully between bed after bed of annuals with flowering trees and shrubs planted right up to the base of the towering walls.

I don't know much about botany, or about the plants' names. I hope they mean more to you than to me. I'm trying to impress you with my feelings rather than with my plant classification knowledge— which I copied from the brochure, anyway.

Now I must stop exuding to give you the economics of this venture. The Butcharts have long passed away, and the project is managed by one of their grandchildren.

It's a money maker, and how! I paid four dollars to view the gardens, and because it is illuminated at night, flower lovers from all over the world can enjoy it every day until 11:00 P.M. From the few inquiries I made, and what I saw myself as hundreds of people streamed through the spacious acres, I would not be surprised if the average attendance is 1,000 a day. That's $40,000. And a restaurant and shops off to the side don't do badly either. I'll let you figure out what this abandoned quarry converted into a garden makes a year. My guess is that it's in seven figures.

So the next time you see an abandoned quarry, take a deep look at it. What happened in North Hollywood and Victoria should make you think. Don't abandon its possibilities too quickly.

HOW A MINI-MALL MET THE SHOPPING NEEDS OF A VANCOUVER SUBURB

Strip shopping developments are out and mini-malls are in. And for a good reason. Mini-mall architecture can more easily be blended with residential surroundings while strip stores can't hide their stark commercial looks. Nowhere have I seen this more dramatically illustrated than in a suburb of Vancouver in British Columbia, Canada.

I was told to see Arbutus Village—a good example of a miniature mall meeting the shopping needs of a residential neighborhood. I drove out to see it. I passed it on the way out, and again when I tried to find it driving back. I looked for a big sign that wasn't there. I was puzzled. I parked near the approximate address, and looking between trees and buildings, I finally spotted a pink brick structure that was somewhat larger than the adjoining homes. I walked close to it, and there it was—"Arbutus Village"—in small letters.

While the outside blended with the adjoining architecture, the inside was a beehive of activity. A foodstore of about 15,000 square feet was obviously its anchor tenant, and about 20 small shops on two levels rounded out the development.

While the architectural treatment was excellent, functionally the planned development left a lot to be desired. Instead of a climate-controlled mall, the planners decided on an open court. While it was pleasant to the eye, it would be unpleasant for shoppers to walk from store to store when it rained or snowed.

I also felt that the planned development would have been more complete if it had a 50-room village motel adjacent to the shopping area so friends, relatives and business associates who come to visit the residents in the area could stay close by, instead of having to drive 10 miles to a downtown hotel. I'm suggesting it because I'm in the process of planning a mini-mall for a suburb of 17,000 people, and I think that a mini-hotel would be an interesting adjunct. That's why I'm thinking it could be feasible for Vancouver too. However, I don't want to leave the impression that I think I'm always right. Remember what I've said elsewhere in these pages—the local developer usually knows substantially more than an outsider. But there's no harm in offering a suggestion. You may want to consider it—in your town.

THE ARCHITECT GOT CARRIED AWAY IN DESIGNING THIS MINI-MALL

Since mini-malls are the real estate rage in this country and Canada, let me conclude with another version of it in Victoria, British Columbia. It's near the heart of downtown and it's known as Nootka Court. The developer converted an old warehouse into a labyrinth of small shops. I use the word labyrinth not so much to describe it, as to connote disapproval. The architecture is pleasant to the eye, but the architect went wild in creating such a maze of pathways and different levels that anyone with a poor sense of direction is sure to get lost. I did.

The little landscaped courts and plazas that wound around the up-and-down shops were cute (not a positive word), but not visible until you got right on top of them. Among the some 20 shops, I saw a fine restaurant, a flower shop, art store, etc., and after viewing them I made my way back to the entrance only to find myself exiting on a different street.

Obviously, the architect and developer tried valiantly to be different, but sometimes being different does not necessarily mean better. Well, this is only one man's opinion. Perhaps people in Victoria have a better sense of direction than I, and don't mind a little wandering in and around and up and down.

The main point of this piece is that mini-malls have taken a firm hold across the length and breadth of the American continent, and you'd be wise to look in on it, if you're looking for a stable real estate investment.

11

How to Build a Big Yearly Real Estate Income In a Small Town

You're living in a large city and you don't like it. You're fed up with congestion, pollution, noise and the rat race. You want out. But how and where? After interviewing dozens of small town inhabitants who've made the move from big city to small town living, here is what I found to be the gist of their experiences.

To do a good job, you've got to tackle this problem with imagination and hard work. You ought not to move to a small town just because a relative or friend moved or lives there. That's not a good enough reason. It's too important a move to rely on serendipity—the hope that somehow it'll turn out right.

Once you've made up your mind to make a major change in your life style—from big city to small town living—you should carefully organize your efforts to choose the right state and right town to suit your particular needs.

Fortunately, there are thousands of lovely small cities, towns and villages to choose from. Take an automobile trip for a couple of weeks and travel the highways and byways (not the freeways) of several states to get the feel of the region. Then pick a state and send for a list of its towns, following it up by a form letter to several dozen Chambers of

Commerce asking for profiles of the towns that appeal to you. Ask for descriptions of their industries, ethnic groups, expansion projections and other questions that interest you.

After you've gotten their replies and picked a half dozen to your liking, take another trip and sample the people of the towns. Talk to bankers, Chamber of Commerce personnel, gasoline station attendants, businessmen—get a more intimate feel of the people. Are they friendly, aloof, cagy, cautious, uninformed, well informed? This personal research is most important. When collated with other statistics, it will enable you to get a more complete picture of the town.

Having selected your town, you're now ready to make your financial move to entrench yourself in it commercially. Depending on your background, you have the following choices: a job with a small manufacturing concern, arranging for a franchise, or buying a small business like a hardware store, gasoline station, restaurant, furniture store, or whatever. The main point, as you're making the transition from big-city to small-town living, is not to think big but to think small—quite a cultural switch from what you've been used to. Remember, this is the reason why you "packed your wagon" in the big city to pioneer this new American frontier. You're among the hundreds of thousands who are doing it, and the exodus will increase as the years roll by.

Once you've rooted yourself in the town of your choice—culturally and financially—you should begin looking for the real estate opportunities which I describe in the following pages.

HOW TO APPLY BIG-CITY REAL ESTATE IDEAS TO SMALL TOWNS

The faster tempo of big-city life does hone the mind, making it more agile. Unfortunately, the agility often turns to city-slicker cunning unless one develops a spiritual philosophy to contain megalopolis expediency. At any rate, big-city experience can be advantageously applied to small towns if ambition is scaled down to a gentler, slower tempo.

For instance, if you left the hustle of a big-city real estate office, where you built, sold, rented or managed hundreds of apartments, don't bring along the rush of big-city organization. Whatever you get into, do it on a small, personalized scale.

Here's what one man did when he left a city of 1,000,000 to settle in a village of 5,000. He converted a 100-year-old woolen-mill factory building into an enclosed mall of 20 small shops.

I drove out to see it. There was big-city imagination mixed with small-town identity. He kept the outside as it was—a mishmash of stone, brick and wooden beams that were filled with patches of gray concrete. A miniature of it in a museum would arouse a lot of interest because of its century old, small-town authenticity. I walked up a few wooden steps into a barny corridor from which radiated a half dozen well lit stores—a silversmith, blacksmith, glass blower, candle maker, wood carver, a winery. The original 100-year-old stairway led to a beehive of second floor shops—fresh baked goodies, unusual china, old armor, antiques, old fashioned candies—all displayed in simple country style. The quaint shopping center had an interesting mix of spotless cleanliness and archaic architecture. And the people who shopped there seemed to meld with the countryish environment— leisurely, conservatively dressed, clean looking.

And now for the real estate economics of the project. The newcomer to the small town not only found the wholesome life he was looking for, but using his big-town savvy, he made several smart moves which insured him a yearly income for the rest of his life.

He bought the woolen mill building for only $50,000, and he was wise not to pour money into changing the outside. He spent it on the inside—where it counted—new electrical wiring, electrical fixtures, heating, plumbing and air conditioning—the life renewal vitals. Altogether, the owner invested about $250,000 and rented 25,000 square feet at $3 a square foot for $75,000.

I don't know the size of his mortgage, but even if he financed it 100 per cent at 10 per cent interest with 20 years amortization, his payments would only be about $30,000 a year. Adding another $20,000 for yearly fixed expenses, I would not be surprised if the owner clears about $25,000 a year. Not bad for a small-town operator who turned his back on big-city living.

"I live at the edge of the village," he told me, "where I watch the play of clouds and changing seasons. I have time to reflect, to look at falling leaves drifting against an azure sky. I have time for a hobby which is making money. I make my own wine and sell it in one of my stores. It's a different world, living out here—quiet, clean, unhurried. Big-city money, impressed with my small-town success, is now trying to entice me back to the big city, but I'd be a fool to succumb to its blandishments. I like it here."

The metropolite who joyously turned "small town," not only used his expertise to provide an adequate income for his family, but he made a contribution to his new community as well. He restored a mass of old brick, stone, and wood into functional use. He was instrumental in starting up several small businesses and providing new goods and services for several thousand townspeople.

THERE'S MONEY IN OLD SMALL-TOWN STOREFRONTS

All right, you bought a hardware store, you leased a gasoline station, or you got a factory or office job in a small-town industrial plant. After you've become acclimated to small-town living, I suggest you begin looking for real estate investment opportunities. They're there if you look in the right places and do the right things. Here is a specific example which with variations can be duplicated in almost every small town in America.

The dusty windows of an empty, two-story furniture store stared blindly on Main Street from a 100 per cent location in a small Wisconsin town. One of the town's inhabitants should have seen its possibilities, but when none did, a big-city real estate adventurer moved in on it. Here's how he developed a $5,000 annuity with practically no money of his own.

He bought the 50 x 100 building for $19,000. The owner was happy to get rid of his liability and the purchaser was happy to buy it. Here's what happened.

One of the savings-and-loan companies was off the beaten path—a few blocks from Main Street, but its board of directors was comfortably set, and probably would not have made a move had it not been for the big-city outsider who showed them a beautiful rendering of what their front and inside offices would look like if they moved into his building. His imaginative selling did the trick. They leased the first floor for ten years at $600 a month—about $1.50 square foot—a bargain by big-city standards. He remodeled the second floor walkup into six apartments and leased them at $145 a unit. His gross rent was close to $18,000 a year.

Now he did a bit of fast-stepping financial borrowing. In addition to his $19,000 initial outlay, he spent $75,000 for remodeling

On the strength of his $18,000-a-year gross rent and about $14,000 net after deducting fixed expenses, he borrowed $90,000 from his main-floor tenant, a safe loan for the savings-and-loan company and a good one for him. Since he had only $4,000 of his own money in the deal, the $5,000-a-year cash flow after debt service on the $90,000 loan, was a good deal indeed. And it was a good deal for the town too—an empty building filled with new life.

"What have you learned," I asked, "working with small town people after a lifetime of big-city experience?"

"Several things. Don't be glib, don't hurry, don't be aggressive. And better get back to old-fashioned honesty—it's still in fashion here."

"And what have you learned from your remodeling project that I can tell my readers?"

"Here's one practical observation. If I had to do it over again, I wouldn't build apartments on the second floor."

"Why not?"

"For several reasons. First, remodeling open space to apartments is much more expensive than converting it to commercial use. And buildings in small towns usually have high ceilings so that a second floor walkup is usually steep. Those extra steps discourage the elderly, the best tenants, from renting the apartments. My cash flow would have been a lot better had I limited my remodeling to the first floor where I spent only $15,000, and rented the upper 5,000 square feet either for storage or cheap office space. That should be of interest to your readers, if they want to get the highest return on their money."

Since there are hundreds of thousands of old store buildings in thousands of small towns in America, the newcomer looking for a yearly income from real estate would do well to analyze the economic insights of this big-city remodeler. With a little imagination and not much money, many small-town buildings losing money could be turned into money makers.

A BIG-CITY IDEA THAT DIDN'T WORK

Bill was big, from a big city and he liked to do things in a big way. One of the things he did was to show 6,000 villagers how things are done where he came from. They taught him a $100,000 lesson he'll long remember.

His first mistake was not to move into the village. His second error was to ignore the difference between the spending habits of big-city and small-town people.

There wasn't one modern office building in the village, and he decided to educate them to new office amenities and big-city spending—at $6 a square foot.

"They'll never pay it," I said when he showed me his plans.

"They will, when they fall in love with the beautiful architecture."

When big Bill finished the 20,000-square-foot office park, it deserved all the "oh's" and "ah's" of those who appreciated unusual design. Instead of an ordinary free-standing building, Bill built three huge white-bricked cottages connected by $25,000 worth of landscaping against a backdrop of trees and a bubbling stream which meandered between and around beautiful walkways. The cost—$600,000.

The first year, Bill leased 15 per cent of the space and lost $65,000. The second year he huffed and puffed into a 40 per cent occupancy and lost $35,000. Now, he's 50 per cent occupied, and still losing money. What was the trouble?

The doctors, lawyers, insurance men, dentists, etc., were not tempted by the titillating beauty of the new office space at $6 a square foot as long as they could remain in their older, comfortable offices at $2 a square foot. Bill discovered that small-towners don't put as much importance on impressing each other as big-city people do. In fact, they seem to take pride in practicing austerity. What Bill didn't know, and he learned it the hard way, was that his well-planned, but nevertheless ostentatious design, discouraged even those who could afford his high rent. They probably were concerned about being considered too citified, a negative characteristic in the eyes of their conservative peers. Whatever the reasons, they combined to cause Bill to lay a big egg.

There's a big lesson to be learned here. Don't try to impose your big-city ideas on small-town people. Rather, learn more about small-town culture, and meld it with big-city know-how in a way that will improve what they have without changing its character. Don't build flamboyantly. Don't remodel ostentatiously. Use big-city ingenuity in devising comfortable shelter at comfortable prices. Merchandise the old charm the way the winery owner did with the old woolen-mill building, described earlier in this chapter.

If you want additional insurance to succeed in building a yearly income in a small town, show them that you appreciate what they have, and they'll respond more favorably to what you have to offer.

BUY A MANY-ACRED MANSION AND DEVELOP THE LAND AROUND IT

Big houses in small towns are becoming as outmoded as mansions in big cities. In the megalopolises, they are torn down and used as skyscraper sites. In small towns, they present opportunities to obtain low-priced land for apartment and commercial development. One of my good friends has done this successfully in some 30 small towns in Wisconsin. Here is the way he did it.

Harold developed three basic plans for building an 8-family, 16-, and 30-family apartment—and with minor variations used one of them to fit the size of the town. At the beginning when he was inexperienced, his land cost was from $2,000 to $3,000 per apartment. He learned to cut it down. Someone offered him a large home on five acres at the edge of town, alongside a river. He bought it for $30,000 with the provision however, that the town was to rezone it for two eight-family sites.

With a bit of friendly help from the seller who knew the town officials, the land was rezoned for 16 units, and the elderly owner got his $30,000—a sum he could never have gotten without the rezoning. Harold advertised the house with an acre of land for $15,000 and sold it immediately. That left him four acres for his 16 apartments, or less than $1,000 a unit cost for land.

Harold wisely built one eight-family to test the market—four one-bedroom units and four two-bedroom units. Within three months after completion, they were all rented at $145 for the smaller flats and $185 for the larger ones.

"Why did they rent so quickly?" I asked Harold.

"For several reasons. First, the edge of town was only a few blocks from the center of Main Street. That offered the tenants a residential setting overlooking a river, yet close to the town's action. Another reason, there were few modern apartments available and there was a strong demand, especially among the elderly who sold or rented their big houses and moved into my cozy, easy to take care of apartments."

"Did you start the second eight right away?"

"Immediately."

"Where did you get the financing?"

"From the local savings-and-loan, and they were so friendly. Even though I was not one of their townsmen, they still applauded my success. And I might add, their interest rate was lower than in the big cities. You see, they don't pay as much for savings, and pass it on to their borrowers."

"Any other hints to help my readers?"

"Yes. Each of my eight-families had a large basement. For a few thousand dollars, I built 1,500 square feet of office space in each, and leased it for $3 a square foot. This added $4,500 a year to the gross income of each building and I don't have to tell you how much that adds to the appraisal value of a property."

"Well, tell us how you came out financially."

"Very well indeed. By saving $1,000 a unit on land and getting $9,000 extra income for office space, I was able to leverage out."

"What do you mean—leverage out?"

"You know that better than I," he laughed. "You wrote the book."

"Explain it to me anyway. I want to see if leverage means the same to you as it does to me."

"Well, an eight-family cost me about $140,000 and I got a loan of about $140,000. I was able to do that because the land appraised for $10,000 more than I paid for it, and I got an extra value credit for my office space of about $10,000, so I had an extra $20,000 going for me. However, I remembered what you said in your *Leverage* book—it's all right to get the maximum loan providing there's a dependable stream of income. Well, I have a dependable stream of income because most of my tenants are retired elderly people who will live out their years in my apartment building."

"Do you have any overage after leveraging out 100 per cent?"

"I was coming to that. I have about $3,000 a year on each eight-family."

This happened in 1971. In 1975 when I checked with Harold to see how he was doing his answer was:

"My cash flow is now $5,000 a year and I can sell each of the eight units for $200,000 anytime I want to."

Is it possible to do as well in 1976-77 with higher interest rates and higher construction costs? I say yes, only if—and it's a big if—you can get the land dirt cheap, for less than $1,000 a unit, and ingeniously cut construction costs. Whatever gap remains will be filled by strong apartment demand and rising rents. Those two conditions will inevitably develop as the present trickle of people moving from big cities to small towns becomes a torrent.

BUY A FARM AND LET IT RIPEN INTO A SUBDIVISION

First—how to buy a farm. Employ the conduit method described in earlier chapters—it's an ideal way to acquire one. After you've spotted a farm that's in the path of growth near a good road, here's how to go about purchasing it.

The chances are that the farm is free and clear, and that the owner is elderly, cautious, and dependent on this asset for his retirement. Let's say it's an 80-acre farm and it's worth $100,000.

Let's suppose you have a good job, good character and you're young—three excellent assets. But you've been able to save only $5,000. That's hardly enough for a down payment.

Go to your local banker and ask for a $5,000 loan. Tell him that you want to use it for a down payment to buy a farm (the chances are the banker will know the owner and the farm). Tell him you intend to move on it and pay off the $90,000 balance on a land contract on a 20-year amortization. Explain the conduit method to the banker—it'll show him you've learned something about creative financing and hopefully, it may impress him enough to lend you the $5,000.

Of course, you'll have to show him how you'll be able to pay it off. Give him a complete analysis of your job earnings, show him how you intend to create a farm income, and most important, convince him that you intend to live frugally within your means. Prepare yourself well. If you can convince the banker to lend you the $5,000, you'll have a good ally in the event you need help to convince the elderly farmer to accept your offer.

The crucial point of the farm deal, of course, is how to explain your offer to the farmer. Expect him to raise both eyebrows when you suggest buying his $100,000 farm with only $10,000 down. And don't be surprised if his wife chimes in with, "That's ridiculous—buying our lifetime work with only $10,000 down."

Your first response to their negative reactions will determine whether you can keep the deal on the track. Something to the effect of, "I don't blame you for being unhappy with my offer," is a good beginning. And, "I don't blame you for wanting all cash," is a good follow-up. But be sure to ask them, "Please be patient and judge my offer after I've had a chance to explain it fully." That ought to at least set the stage for their listening attention.

Now, after having had the practice of explaining the conduit method to the banker, it should flow smoother explaining it to them. By all means, speak slowly and clearly. For instance, explain how they gain by selling to you on a land contract as contrasted to selling for cash, and conclude in this manner; "Uncle Sam doesn't want you to evade taxes, but it's perfectly legal to avoid them if the government allows it."

Spend a little time explaining how difficult it is to sell for cash today—how mortgage money is practically unavailable on vacant land. Then make the strongest point of all—promise solemnly that you intend to make the $90,000 land-contract balance the most sacred obligation of your life, because meeting the payments on time involves the future welfare of two families: "Yours, because you would depend upon me for your livelihood; and mine, because if I don't make the payments, my family, farm and future would be at stake."

After you've slowly and carefully made your explanations and promises, be sure you add:

"I don't want you to consider this offer seriously until you have me explain it to your lawyer, your banker or whomever you trust as an advisor. This is a big move for you and you should think it over carefully."

If they invite you to explain the deal to their lawyer or family advisor, you've taken an important step. Your success will depend more on the impact your character will have on him, than the commercial analysis of the deal. If you have a tendency to be aggressive—restrain yourself—don't become voluminous with your explanations. Your most telling argument could be that the banker, whom their advisor will no doubt know, had agreed to advance $5,000 toward the down payment of the deal. This will serve a double purpose. It'll show him you're honest—you've divulged a cash weakness—and he may check out the deal with the banker whom you've already won over on your side.

Preparing for a college examination isn't nearly as important as preparing yourself to explain the conduit method. Be sure you understand it thoroughly, and then give it your all—like your future depended upon it—because it could.

HOW BIG-CITY FINANCING SECURES
A YOUNG MAN'S FUTURE
IN A SMALL TOWN

Joel was a shrewd real estate operator. He left his small town years ago to make his mark in the big city, and he did. He got his degree in financing on the firing line of action. He scrambled near the top of the heap. His three grown sons, however, didn't have his shrewdness or interests. One took a government job, and another became a professor. The third would be content to leave the big city to make a small mark in some small town. But how and where?

His father gave him the answer. Joel was smart enough to know that his third son could not do what he did, nor would he be happy doing it. He began looking for a real estate deal that would anchor his youngest son in a small town with a yearly income. It didn't take Joel long to find it.

Being of a practical rather than philosophical nature, the father was more interested in a good project than a good town. Fortunately, he found it in a town his son liked. It had a population of 10,000 and near its center was an old, 100-room hotel, bar and restaurant. It was being advertised for sale at $260,000 by the owner.

Joel made a quick analysis of the deal. Several small, modern motels on the outskirts had siphoned off most of the business from the outdated hotel. Joel knew that the owner was having problems making payments on his $150,000 first and $20,000 second mortgages. Joel told the owner he would be interested, but at a price below the first mortgage. That, of course, ended their negotiations.

Several months later, Joel received a telephone call from a bank official who held the $150,000 first mortgage on the hotel. "Are you still interested in buying the hotel?"

"The only way I'd be interested, is to buy your mortgage at a discount," Joel told the official. "You and the owner have a white elephant on your hands. You know it, he knows it, and unfortunately for the two of you, I know it."

"Well, I guess there's nothing to talk about then," the banker replied.

"I guess not, unless you want to take a loss on your mortgage," Joel concluded.

A month later, the banker called again.

"Will you drive in to see us. Let's talk."

"I'll be glad to."

Foreclosure proceedings against the hotel had already started. Joel detected a reluctance on the part of the bank to become involved in managing a loser. For all practical purposes, the owner had already been wiped out. Now the bank wanted out and Joel knew it. He drove a hard bargain. But it was between equals. The bank made a bad loan and there was no way out except to take a loss. Joel bought the $150,000 first mortgage for $75,000 in cash and stepped into the bank's shoes.

In checking the abstract records, Joel found that the $20,000 second mortgage had been, for some reason, recorded ahead of the first. That information helped Joel strike a hard bargain with the bank, and he wasted no time in going to the second mortgagee and buying his $20,000 mortgage for $10,000. Apparently the holder of the second mortgage wasn't aware that his was first and Joel wasn't about to tell him. (I might suggest here that Joel should have told him. He could have been a moral as well as a financial hero).

Joel had a mere $85,000 invested in the hotel when the foreclosure ripened for bidding. But the total debts against it were over $200,000, including the $150,000 first, $20,000 second, foreclosure costs and delinquent taxes. No one bid, and Joel wound up with the property for less than $100,000.

But that's only the beginning of the story. Joel was as adept in handling his son as he was in acquiring the hotel. This is what he told him:

"This building will never make it as a hotel. The new motels have knocked it out of competition. But it can make it as a small apartment project. I've done my job. Now you've got to do yours. I want you and your wife to move into the hotel and take charge of remodeling. Get a local architect, a list of plumbers, electricians, carpenters, painters, etc., and start getting bids. This will acquaint you with the townspeople. I'm not going to meddle, but if you spend more than $100,000 for converting the 100 rooms into 30 apartments, I'll know you've been taken. If you see it's coming in at more than your budget, tell the contractors to sharpen their pencils. Stress function, eliminate frills."

"Did it come in at less than $100,000?" I asked.

"You bet. It was a tussle, but he made it. And he did a good job in renting. I should say, they did—his wife pitched in too."

"What happened to the bar and restaurant?"

"That almost caused a rift between us. I wanted John (his son) to run it. It did a good business, but John is a softie. He felt sorry for the previous owner who lost the property, and leased it to him at a ridiculously low rental so he could make a living."

When I pried deeper into the economics of the deal, I found that Joel got a new mortgage of $200,000 after the remodeling was completed, and had his son sign it. The gross rent was $70,000 and fixed expenses and debt service about $50,000. With no money of his own, Joel created a yearly income for his son of $20,000. Since John ostensibly did all the work on the project, he became somewhat of an overnight hero in his town. His father's masterminding was the invisible part of the deal.

Not every young man who wants to move to a small town has a father like Joel, but every town has opportunities similar to the one I've described. It's up to you to spot them, analyze them and make the improvisations to fit the town, your abilities, and your needs.

I hope these examples and insights will help you do it. Good luck!

12

It's Good Business to
Think Beyond Profit

The idealists have been the practical men of every age. Short-range practicality that isn't linked to idealism eventually degenerates into expediency and corruption.

The elderly, the retarded, the sick, use more than they produce. The healthy and wealthy produce more than they use. Unless the "haves" help the "have nots," a community, no matter what its political system, soon disintegrates into a chaos of impractical selfishness. So, in addition to building a big yearly continuing income, I'd like to suggest that we devote some time to idealism—the winners helping the losers. As you will see, in helping the losers, neighborhoods are upgraded and real estate values go up. Both the winners and losers win.

A UNIQUE REMODELING IDEA
SAVES THE PUBLIC $500,000

Let me trace a series of beyond-profit incidents which gave 50 infants a chance for normal development, and at the same time saved the public $500,000.

A professor of social work in one of our urban universities became acutely aware that many children from one to five years old, with various defects, were further misshapen by home neglect. Mongoloids, the retarded, and babies of raped mothers (he knew of one such mother who was 12 years old) wallowed in homes without proper care and without love. As a social scientist, he knew how high the cost would be to the community in future years if nothing was done to help these helpless children during the critical, formative, one-to-five years.

Two of his students in graduate school had a feel for helping problem children. Their interest fused them into marriage. The professor got an idea.

"Why don't you start a Montessori School?" (Maria Montessori was an Italian doctor who developed unusual ideas to treat unusual children.)

"What are we going to use for money? Where can we teach?" the young couple asked.

"I'll help you get the money, if you find a place to teach."

The two young social workers started with several children in a church basement with the money the professor got from a small county grant. They cared for the children from 9 a.m. to 3 p.m., five days a week. The mothers were delighted, the children responded, the couple was quickened, and the professor was rewarded. His idea took root. Soon it began to sprout. He formed a board of directors to supervise the school's activities and in time, it began to bloom. That's when I came in.

When I attended the first board meeting, I saw that the professor knew what he was doing. As I looked around the room, I recognized a local banker, an accountant, a labor leader, several black women, and a half dozen socialites. Why did he pick me, I wondered? I soon found out.

"George," the professor cornered me after one of the board meetings, "we need a school. I'm banking on you to get it for us."

It was a big order. There were 50 children between one and five and 30 teachers (some volunteers) who were trying to make the best of the cramped basement quarters. I visited the children several times.

"This little boy," one of the teachers was telling me as she showed me through the dreary classrooms, "was a vegetable when we enrolled him. He failed to respond physically or emotionally to us or to any of the other children. After three months, he reached out for a toy. We celebrated—it was a big event in his life and in our school.

Gradually, his responses increased and now he plays almost normally with the other children."

I looked at the little boy and the other little tots who were so completely dependent on the teachers' love and understanding for their tiny toeholds on life—and I decided to get that school for them.

It wasn't easy. There were no capital funds available from the county for private agencies. We needed about a 15,000 square foot school, and I knew it would cost about $850,000 to build, including the land. That amount was out of the question. We could never raise it. But $350,000? Maybe.

I started looking for old buildings which could be remodeled into a school—mansions, garages, abandoned stores or factory buildings. Wrong location, price, and code requirements eliminated a half dozen right away.

Then I chanced on a vacant two story building of about 20,000 square feet that had been a bowling alley. The location was right, the structure was sound and the $125,000 price was in line. But it faced a very busy street. Its front was in a shambles—three skid-row stores on one side, and two boarded-up stores on the other—a picture of shameful neglect. I turned it down. During the next several months, nothing better turned up. The board of directors waited for my miracle. I felt I was letting down the professor, the board, and especially the children.

I went back to the vacant bowling alley. It still looked as bad, and the street was as congested as ever. My mind still said no. I drove away, turning down the residential street behind the bowling alley. Then I suddenly stopped the car, struck by an idea. There I was in front of dilapidated rooming house whose 50 x 180 foot lot abutted the bowling alley to its rear. Why not build a front entrance at the rear of the bowling alley where there was little noise or traffic, tear down the old rooming house, and make a playground out of the lot? The more I thought about it, the more I liked it.

I went to work. A savings-and-loan company had foreclosed its $400,000 mortgage on the building ten years ago, and it had been vacant ever since. Using my profit-motive expertise and non-profit zeal, I persuaded the savings-and-loan company to sell their vacant "loser" to Montessori for $85,000 with $10,000 down, and the balance on a land contract with the entire amount due and payable in two years. I also optioned the rooming house for $25,000.

The board reluctantly approved both purchases after I 'guesstimated' that we could raze the rooming house, build a playground and remodel 15,000 square feet of the 20,000 square foot structure for $250,000 into a first-class school. Several board members raised legitimate questions.

"What happens if we can't raise the $350,000 to pay for the buildings and the remodeling? What do we do with the real estate then?"

One socialite board member whose heart was as big as her husband's fortune said, "We can do it if Mr. Bockl's figures are right. Just think, we can have our close-to-a-million-dollar school for only $350,000!" That turned the vote in favor of the project.

I hired an architectural firm that had just completed remodeling an old loft building into a beautiful bank. I said: "I want good design and durable function at the lowest possible cost. Review all possible materials. It's got to come in at close to $250,000. This is a greater architectural challenge than the bank job. There, money was no object. Here, money must control all your decisions. Yet, I want a school that will answer the children's needs. And I might add—we might as well start by cutting your fee to the least you can live with. That's going to set an example for all the subcontractors."

The total remodeling bids came in slightly above $300,000. I went to work on each of the subcontractors, and using the charitable argument as well as making some minor changes that didn't hurt the project, I whittled them down to about $275,000.

The remodeling and fund raising began at the same time. The socialite women on the board took on the work of soliciting the Who's Who of our city, the banker arranged loans to pay the contractors, the accountant kept track of the building expenditures, and the labor leader issued statements commending the project. When the remodeling was finished the women had raised $350,000 in cash and pledges, as remarkable a feat as getting an $850,000 school built for slightly over $375,000.

Here is a shining example of people helping people. It all started with an ideal in a professor's head, and as a result, hundreds of youngsters will be given a chance for a normal life, and millions of dollars of public money will be saved.

The austere real estate principle which made this worthwhile project possible should be used creatively in many public projects. We must be as imaginative in spending public money as the private enterprisers are when they're building for profit. In these times of material shortages and capital scarcity, the needy will be neglected unless the idealists come up with low cost, practical solutions.

Aside from the altruism of helping the needy children, converting the blighted bowling alley into a modern school gave a lift to the immediate neighborhood. It boosted values of the adjacent properties and had the effect of inducing others to modernize.

IRREVERENCE FOR PUBLIC MONEY COSTS HOSPITAL $10,000,000

Unfortunately, our minds are easily caught by catch phrases.

"Go first class or don't go at all," was one of the aphorisms our hospital consultant used in 1970 when he advised us (the board of directors) on our next move for the development of our hospital.

The expert presented us with three options:

(1) Spend $6,000,000 renovating about 100 of the 250 rooms, and modernize the radiology and surgery departments.

(2) Spend $10,000,000 and add a hundred new rooms in addition to the $6,000,000 first option expenditure.

(3) Spend $20,000,000 by buying a square block of land across the street and build about 75 per cent of a new hospital there, connecting it with the old one via a street over-head and underground tunnel.

"Of course," the expert concluded, "I strongly recommend the third option."

While he was talking, my mind was flashing with an idea which I thought was superior to any of his options. First, let me tell you how the idea came about and then describe his reaction to it.

While attending a seminar several months previous to this meeting, I became friendly with the chairman of a committee in charge of development in a hospital located five blocks from ours. After exchanging a few remarks about boards' responsibilities in running hospitals, he said:

"I know that your board is about to launch a campaign to raise money to renovate your hospital. We've already done it and we're not so sure it was the right move. We've just finished spending $10,000,000 in the wrong location. We should have built a smaller hospital on the far west side where most of our patients and doctors live."

"It's not too late," I said only half facetiously. "Let *us* buy your hospital."

"That's not a bad idea."

I pursued it more seriously.

"Do you think your board of directors would consider moving after being in the central part of the city for three quarters of a century?"

"It comes up at meetings many times, but the stopper is always—what do we do with the present hospital?"

"Well, now you might have your answer."

I spent an entire afternoon going through my new found friend's hospital. They spent the $10,000,000 on a new, adjacent building, housing 200 new beds, several ancillary departments, and a foundation to take 12 additional floors for up to 1,000 beds. By adding another $6,000,000 to this building, plus what they had in their adjoining buildings, we could have all we were going to have in our $20,000,000 addition and our own older buildings. There was another great plus in their hospital complex. They had parking for about 700 cars. We would have to spend another $2,000,000 for additional parking.

I became excited about saving our hospital $10,000,000. But I had to do a little homework first. I called a member of the board of a small, antiquated hospital who was looking for a larger facility. I took him through our hospital, and within several weeks, he reported that their board would be willing to consider buying it for $6,000,000 with $1,000,000 in cash as a down payment.

I went to the president of our hospital and told him about my plans. At first he smiled benignly.

"You know the board would never vote to sell our hospital and move to another. We've got too much tradition, too much history here."

"Even if we save $10,000,000?"

"Well, let's take a look at it."

After he, a few key members of our board and I spent several hours viewing the new $10,000,000 addition, their older buildings and parking facilities, the president said:

"Let's find out what they want for it."

I did. Their board met and agreed to sell their hospital for $11,000,000. Our president then arranged a meeting with our consultant to discuss the advisability of purchasing the other hospital and the sale of ours. After he listened to my story, he said:

"I've seen the other hospital buildings from the outside. They're completely inadequate. If we want to go first class, considering this exchange will only lead to a waste of time and a delay in planning."

That impressed my president, but not me. When we were alone he said:

"Well that should end it. We're paying him $150,000 and he certainly ought to know."

"Will you do me a favor?" I asked the president. "Let me present the $10,000,000 savings plan to the board."

"All right," he said, "if you insist.'

I explained my plan in detail. I was fair. I stressed the negatives—moving away from tradition, less attractive architecture than what we were planning, and several departments not arranged exactly the way we would have liked. But I zeroed in on the main, positive point—having almost all we wanted for $10,000,000 less!

The board was not impressed. I had indeed, wasted my time. The consultant's, "Go first class, or not at all," sunk in too deeply. The board wanted their own planning, not someone else's. It was a luxury they didn't want to give up.

"Even if it costs $10,000,000 more?" I questioned insistently.

"Yes, even if it costs $10,000,000 more."

But that was in 1971. By the time we started building, it was late 1973. The stock market had begun plunging and interest rates soaring. And in 1976, as our hospital addition was being completed, the $20,000,000 original cost increased to $24,000,000.

To add to our woes, our hospital occupancy dropped from 85 to 68 per cent. And the hospital we should have bought (I still cling to my opinion) had only a 50 per cent occupancy. The public which is called upon to subsidize these hospitals, can't afford the pride of tradition or the need for competition that now exists between hospitals. Had we bought the neighboring hospital for $11,000,000, we would have had a higher occupancy, a lower debt service by $10,000,000 and lower costs to patients. Perhaps the architecture of the other hospital would not have been as monumental as our architecture, but neither would our budget be straining and overflowing in the red.

We need more reverence for austerity, not tradition; for lower priced medical service, not more denominational identity; for higher occupancy rates, not more competition among hospitals. We need to treat eleemosynary money with a great deal of respect and responsibility, even more than the money which generates the profit that makes public funds available. As Benjamin Franklin used to say, "Ere fancy you consult, consult your purse."

IF YOU DON'T BEND WITH THE TIMES, THEY'LL BREAK YOU

Having lost my bid to make a three-way hospital move to save $10,000,000, I gracefully abided by the overwhelming majority, and plunged into the building activities of my hospital to see if I could save money elsewhere. I quickly ran into another major difference of opinion.

Our board of directors authorized the purchase of a five-story, 60,000 square foot school building adjoining the new addition of our hospital. It was about 50 years old but in excellent condition. When we decided to add a medical office building to our addition, our consultant decided that the old school building would be the ideal site. Without a second thought, he advised that the school be razed at a cost of $100,000, and a new 60,000 square foot medical office structure be built at a cost of $2,250,000.

"It'll pay for itself," he told the board.

"I'd like to differ with you again, sir," I said. "It won't pay for itself. You'd have to get $9.50 a square foot to come out even, and the doctors won't pay it. This is something I know. I've dealt with about a hundred of them on a landlord-tenant basis, and I know how they think. They're not going to give up their present $4 a square foot space and pay $9.50 just to be near their hospital."

"What do you suggest?" he asked impatiently.

"That we spend about $500,000 remodeling the school building and charge $4.50 a square foot. Then you'll fill it, and the hospital won't have to subsidize it."

"How will it look—an old eyesore next to a beautiful edifice?'

"It can be blended, with a little imagination. When the old gray brick is sandblasted, it may have more character than some of the new exterior materials used today."

"Well," he said with a tone of finality, "I don't recommend it."

Concerned about our escalating costs, this time the board listened to the voice of frugality. But it didn't go all the way. I wanted to leave the corridors of the old school as they were. The distance from hallway to outside window was about 23 feet—the ideal for office layout. I suggested carpeting throughout, lowering ceilings, flush lighting, two new passenger elevators, vinyl for hallway walls and offices, new front, and leaving the beautiful, textured, gray brick intact—except for sandblasting it.

The consultant would not have it this way. He retreated from his new $2,250,000 building position to gutting the entire inside, removing the outside brick and covering it with material to blend with the new hospital addition. The cost of this like-new renovation was about $1,250,000. And the rent—to come out even—would have to be $7.50 per square foot. I objected to stripping the building down to the skeleton for an extra $750,000, but I was overruled.

The medical building was finished in late 1973, and by the end of 1974, it was only 40 per cent occupied. Why? The doctors on the staff refused to pay $7.50 a square foot when they were comfortably located nearby for $4 a square foot. The hospital lost $125,000 on its office building that year. After appealing to their loyalty and giving them "deals," a few more doctors moved in. At the end of 1975, the hospital's medical building was still 40 per cent vacant, and it lost about $75,000.

Had we spent only $500,000 for remodeling and charged $4 a square foot, I'm sure the building would have been filled within six months, and the hospital would not have lost a dime. So what if the hallways were a bit labyrinthine? The patients would have found their way to the doctors anyway. And what's so bad about sandblasted bricks that still had a century of life in them? Many, I among them, think they would have had more charm than the monotonous brown, prefabricated exterior that replaced them.

We'll have to learn more quickly how to make the transition from affluence to austerity. New York City learned it too slowly and is on the verge of bankruptcy. Our hospital, still steeped in the syndrome of going first class, is squirming financially, and desperately needs several million dollars of donations from the private sector to rescue it from its profligacy.

We have a more sober board now. The free-spending consultant is no longer with us. Our main concern now is not more spending, but where to cut to stay financially afloat.

In the years ahead, whether we flail away in profit making or labor in the non-profit sector, let's remember that frugality is still a great virtue, and trampling on it is a vice, no matter how we clothe it with respectability.

There's an unerring law of cause and effect. In the East, it's known as the law of Karma; in the West, Ralph Waldo Emerson described it in his famous essay, *Compensation*. Whether it's a family, a hospital, a city or a nation, when it spends beyond its means, the reckoning is as sure as day follows night.

It's wiser to bend with frugality than be broken by profligacy.

BUILD A RETIREMENT VILLAGE FOR PROFIT AND TURN IT OVER TO A NON-PROFIT ASSOCIATION

Here is a happy mixture of building a friendship village for the elderly and a yearly income for yourself. It's an idea still in its early stages, but it's going to sweep the country. It's good for you, and for those who need it.

Here's how it works. Option a scenic site of several acres, either in a small town or large city near shopping and social activity, yet secluded from the hubbub. Then select a good architect to draw preliminary plans for 100 to 200 apartments depending on the size of the site and the town. It should not be difficult with the help of a reputable contractor to arrive at an approximate cost. Be sure to add interest, taxes and other miscellaneous costs during the course of construction. When you've accounted for all the loose ends so that you have a realistic cost for the project, add another 5 per cent for good measure, and present it to the lender for a mortgage.

Before we get into the intricacies of financing, let me offer a few suggestions about the special amenities and services the friendship village should offer.

Let's assume you've decided on 100 apartments. Whether you build an elevatored tower or a cluster of one-story cottages surrounding the public areas, you should vary the size of the units to include studios and one-bedroom units with a sprinkling of two-bedroom apartments for couples. The inclusion of balconies is a must. The public areas should consist of a main lounge, sunroom, restaurant, greenhouse, crafts room, library, a large meeting and party room, and a dozen rooms set aside for nursing care. In addition to the physical amenities, the following services should be offered: complete nursing care when necessary, recreational programs, three meals a day, maid service and push button alert from apartment to nurse at all times.

After you've refined your plans, you should arrange to present your idea to a non-profit board of directors who will manage this elderly housing project. It could be a church, a hospital or a group of civic-minded men and women who would supervise the project on an eleemosynary basis.

Having arranged for a temporary construction loan and a board of directors to oversee the completed project, you should now develop a marketing plan to pay off the cost of the project. Let's assume its total cost is $1,300,000. You should sell the units so they average $15,000 each for a total of $1,500,000. This will leave a $200,000 cushion for future contingencies. Do not start building until you've pre-sold at least 50 apartments. The pre-building sales kit should contain the following information:

First, a beautiful, colored rendering of the project and a picture as well as a floor plan of each type of apartment. In bold type, state the price for a studio, one bedroom and two bedroom unit, and in still bolder type, the monthly service fee for each. Then in easy to understand language, state what the residents will be getting for their monthly fees. The brochure should answer questions like these:

> Question: Is the price of an apartment and the use of all the ancillary facilities the same for one who is 62 and another who is 82?
>
> Answer: The price will differ with age. Upon death, your apartment will revert to the non-profit association and can be resold. However, should you wish to move any time during the first eight years of your residency, you will receive a declining refund.

Question: Is there extra charge for nursing when one becomes ill?

Answer: No. Professional nursing care is provided without additional cost. Of course, you'll have to pay your private physician, but most of the fee would be covered by Medicare.

Question: Why the monthly service charge?

Answer: To cover the operational costs such as meals, maids, nursing, maintenance, administration, etc.

Question: What if the monthly service charge is raised and I can't afford it, or if I run out of money and can't even pay the original monthly fee?

Answer: You'll not have to move. You'll be subsidized out of an emergency fund created from the resale of apartments due to attrition.

Question: Who will own the project?

Answer: A non-profit corporation run by a Board of Directors who serve without pay. They supervise the staff to see that professional care is provided and that the owners' interests are protected.

Obviously, there can be many variations to this general plan. Prices for lifelong use of apartments could vary from $10,000 to $30,000 and monthly service fees from $150 to $450, depending on how modest or luxurious the complex.

The sponsors or non-profit associations vary also. In Madison, Wisconsin, a group who call themselves Attic Angels are sponsors of an Angel Tower, the first retirement facility in that city catering to the average and above-average incomes. In Milwaukee, a very successful life-care living complex is known as Friendship Village, and consists of 288 garden apartments on 15 beautiful wooded acres, located less than a mile from the largest enclosed shopping center in Wisconsin.

And an elegant mansion in Montecito, south of Santa Barbara, California, formed the nucleus of an $11,000,000 retirement community that is comparable to the finest resort in the world. The selling price starts at $22,500 and the monthly service charge, from $420 and up. Cottages, garden apartments and townhouses are clustered around the beautiful mansion, connected with walkways amidst its 48 acres of luxurious gardens. As an added precaution, the reserve funds created from the entry fees are supervised by the State Department of Health to assure each resident of his purchased rights.

You should now have a pretty good idea how retirement villages are conceived and carried to completion. If you option a site for 100 units, draw plans, arrange for interim financing, prepare a marketing program, build the project and form a non-profit association to supervise it—what should you get for all your labors? Don't walk away with a $100,000 fee. By the time you're through with federal and perhaps state taxes, you may be left with only $40,000. That's not enough. And paying the $100,000 fee at the start might prove a hardship to the project. I suggest you negotiate for a $12,500 annuity for 25 years. That would be much better for you, and ought not be financially burdensome to a well-conceived friendship village project.

But the biggest part of your reward will be that which transcends profit—a wholesome feeling of being responsible for creating a pleasant and secure way of life for a hundred elderly people who will bless you for the rest of their days.

RECYCLING BUILDINGS IS CONSERVING ENERGY

Material and energy shortages have become crucial problems. That is why reusing used products is not just a good idea—it's a grim necessity.

And that's why recycling old buildings into new uses makes a lot of energy-saving sense. Remodeling used buildings can make a tremendous contribution to conservation because it could save society millions of tons of material and the equivalent of trillions of barrels of oil and watts of electricity. Here's a recap of some of my remodeling viewed from the standpoint of conservation rather than profit.

A six story, 100,000 square foot warehouse was gathering dust. The reason—the methods of warehousing had changed and so did the neighborhood. The vacant building was a liability to the owner and

prospective buyers were eyeing it for razing. The demolition would
have cost about $100,000 of energy. To reproduce the huge, poured
concrete structure would have cost $1,000,000. I spent $1,200,000
converting it into a modern medical office building. Had I built it
new, it would have cost $2,200,000, and I would have had to use an
additional $1,000,000 worth of energy.

And that was not the only saving. I used less credit, kept inflation and interest rates down, met tenants' needs at lower rentals,
shored up a slipping neighborhood and increased the city's tax base.

* * *

Seventy-five years ago, the six story, 50,000 square foot Steinmeyer Building was a farmers' mecca for trading their produce for
groceries. Now, it was about to be scrapped. Nobody wanted it. The
smell of coffee grindings of decades ago still permeated the dank air
of its upper floors. Some saw it as a future land site. I saw it as a
commercial home for printers, artists and low-priced office users.

I bought it for $130,000, spent $70,000 for remodeling and filled
it with artists, printers, insurance companies and social agencies with
budget problems. The Wisconsin Heart Association enjoyed a low,
one-dollar-a-square-foot rental for over a decade.

Had the Steinmeyer Building been razed, its present tenants
would have had to find offices elsewhere, eventually necessitating the
construction of new space at higher prices. Saving it conserved tons o
steel, cement and lumber—and perhaps enabled those with limited
budgets to remain in business. And that's not all. A landmark
building was preserved for many more years of productive life.

* * *

The northwest corner of Seventh Street and Wisconsin Avenu
in my city used to house an automobile agency. It was vacant, an
next to a partially occupied building. Both buildings were owned b
the same person, and both presented a forlorn picture of neglecte
rejected, and uncared for real estate. Oil slicks still marked the
wooden floors. A real estate broker offered them for sale.

"Hold on to 'em, 'til a big company wants a downtown buildi
site," he urged, "and you'll make a killing."

But his sales pitch didn't strike a responsive chord. I was thinking of the Steinmeyer Building. Here was a better location. Why not duplicate my success?

I did. I sanded out the oil slicks, covered them with asphalt tile, joined the two buildings with a passenger elevator, lowered ceilings, built partitions and leased the entire 60,000 square feet to lawyers, insurance companies, labor organizations, etc. for $1.50 a square foot. The Milwaukee Bucks had their offices there for a number of years. I have subsequently sold it and the present owner is still grossing over $100,000 a year.

Again, energy was saved, an important downtown corner shored up and tenants who were not interested in luxury, found comfortable commercial space at a comfortable price.

* * *

Several years ago, I made a stab at a miniature Trolly Square (discussed elsewhere in this book) when I offered to purchase two huge car barns on ten acres of land. It didn't materialize because the $1,000,000 asking price for the site was five times as high proportionately as the Trolly Square land. My mini-mall idea was blocked by high land costs. The wrecking ball won out. Tons of in-place material turned to dust when these barns were pulverized.

* * *

Thousands of man hours, tons of cement and hundreds of thousands of board feet of lumber went into the sturdy Cutler-Hammer Building on North Water a few blocks south of Milwaukee's City Hall. Several years ago, this 200,000 square foot vacant building was offered to me for a song, but I didn't know what to do with it. While I was searching for a recycling idea, a bank bought it and razed it.

Were it available today, I would know what to do with it because of what I read about a 250,000 square foot piano factory in Boston which was recycled into 174 apartments at a profit to the entrepreneur and low rents to the tenants. I too, could have converted the sound 200,000 square foot building into 150 apartments and saved our country several million dollars worth of energy and materials.

* * *

About 20 years ago, the Bresler Building on North Milwaukee Street was vacant except for a corner used by Bresler Galleries. While others were eyeing it for razing, I fell in love with its charm—a circular stairway leading to a Florentine-tiled second floor, decorative wrought-iron outside balconies, a 20-foot high, third floor ballroom that would cost $500,000 to duplicate.

My real estate associates chided me for buying a white elephant when I paid $125,000 for it. I enhanced its charm by making a few cosmetic changes. I antiqued the 12-foot entrance door and washed off 20 years of grime from the second and third floor woodwork to bring it back to its original beauty. All the building needed was a good scrubbing. I spent only $20,000. I retained Bresler Galleries, leased the other store to a carpet company, interested a commercial artist in renting the second floor, and got a dance studio for the third floor. After resuscitating the building I sold it at a good profit.

It's still being used today, providing an excellent return for the owner. To have razed it would have been a colossal waste of energy—something we can no longer afford.

* * *

A group of buildings along the Milwaukee River, in the heart of our downtown could wind up in rubble and a parking lot unless someone with a feel for conservation saves them. They would make an interesting Stonecroft (discussed elsewhere in this book)—a European idea which could be applied to any row of old buildings. A mix of imagination and money could transform these forlorn looking structures into a charming development of living quarters up and stores down. The difference between putting the wrecking ball to them and what I'm proposing is either having another ugly parking lot or a charming cluster of low cost, newly painted, colorful buildings—and again, saving tens of thousands of tons of steel, hundreds of thousands of bricks, and millions of board feet of lumber. There's no reason why many of our 50-year-old buildings should not go on sheltering people for the next 100 years, as in Switzerland, where a building that's 100 years old is still in its prime.

The age of unlimited energy and material is over. Our throwaway habits must be extirpated. How long are the people who are sharing the planet Earth with us going to tolerate America's using 40 per cent of the world's yearly energy for 6 per cent of the world's population? It's irresponsible and immoral. And we had better do something about it.

Why can't we, the leading country in energy use, become the leader in conserving it? There are countless ways we can do it, and recycling buildings is one of them.

For an outstanding example of resuscitating old buildings I recommend that you become acquainted with what Seattle, Washington did in revitalizing Pioneer Square.

A NEW WAY TO REVITALIZE AMERICA'S DOWNTOWNS

The decay of our downtowns will not be reversed by new skyscraper hotels, huge shopping centers or high-rise apartment complexes. They're not only economically unfeasible today, they would actually speed up the decay of the remaining stock of downtown properties.

We're in a new real estate ball game. The age of bigness has ended. It has been tried and found wanting. New York already knows it. The evidence is in—its new multi-million dollar skyscrapers did not eliminate the adjacent blight—the blight enveloped the skyscrapers. The worshipers of bigness are paying through the nose—25 per cent of the glass and steel sky giants are now vacant and foreclosures are rife. With some variations, this is true of every large American city.

What's the solution?

Let's not fall into New York's trap. Instead of adding new skyscrapers, why not recycle our stock of old downtown buildings—where decay begins and spreads. Horizontal redevelopment with extensive recycling of buildings, making small additions where feasible, is far more practical in eliminating decay than vertical development, which leaves the adjacent blight intact. What good is it to build a multi-million dollar, 30-story giant on half a square block, and let a dozen adjacent blocks stew in their decay? It doesn't make sense, especially when we see what it has done to dozens of cities across the nation.

If the *Milwaukee Journal* in my city had abandoned its 50-year-old building 20 years ago and built a new skyscraper, it would have contributed to Milwaukee's blight. By adding some new to the old, it stopped decay in its tracks and turned Journal Square into an aesthetic architectural showpiece where the old blends with the new.

Conversely—with the best of intentions—the First Wisconsin National Bank left a beautiful but empty, 50-year-old building behind when it built the new 42-story Wisconsin Center a half mile away. Unless the now half-empty building can be imaginatively put to good use, it will become a new seedbed of blight which will spread to other buildings.

Instead of planning new big buildings and neglecting the old, we should develop a master downtown plan to recycle what we have. We can more pervasively change downtown's landscape by creating dozens of new Stonecrofts, imaginatively converting factory buildings into living quarters, garages into mini-malls and loft buildings into comfortable, low-priced office space. Such horizontal restoration should be punctuated by small parks and open spaces. The cost of such redevelopment of several square miles would probably be less than building one huge hotel on a half square block. And it would be far more meaningful—sociologically and economically.

It's been said that half our population is engaged in manufacturing goods, and the other half in selling them to each other. Let's not sell them in huge selling factories where scanners and mechanical devices depersonalize relationships; but in small shops in small old and new buildings, where there may be less efficiency but more personal relationships.

A downtown that's alive with hundreds of small merchants in renovated buildings may be less efficient, but it'll be more livable. And what's more, it'll arrest downtown blight—a dread disease that debilitates buildings and people.

It so happens that the altruism of uplifting needy people, and the patriotism of recycling old buildings, could help reverse the plummeting of real estate values wherever blight infects a neighborhood. Let's coin an adage, "What's good for people is good for real estate." When we do the right and wise thing, real estate values go up. When we don't, we suffer the reverse.

We need new real estate thinking. I urge my readers to translate some of these ideas into action—for profit and beyond profit.

Index

OTHER REAL ESTATE INVESTMENT AND SELLING BOOKS FROM <u>REWARD</u> THAT YOU WON'T WANT TO MISS!

- ☐ 16751-0 **Confident Selling,** James R. Fisher, Jr. — $4.95
- ☐ 27618-8 **Encyclopedia of Real Estate Forms,** Jerome S. Gross — $12.95
- ☐ 35483-7 **Getting Through to People,** Jesse S. Nirenberg — $4.95
- ☐ 43110-6 **How Real Estate Fortunes Are Made,** George Bockl — $4.95
- ☐ 40303-0 **How to Build a Fortune Investing in Land,** John E. Kirk — $3.95
- ☐ 40944-1 **How to Get Rich in Real Estate,** Robert W. Kent — $3.95
- ☐ 40978-9 **How to Go From Rags to Riches Fast With Sound Real Estate Investments,** J. Brad Lampley — $3.95
- ☐ 41864-0 **How to Make High Profits in Apartment Investments,** Harry J. Greene — $9.95
- ☐ 41850-9 **How to Make One Million Dollars in Real Estate in Three Years, Starting with No Cash,** Tyler G. Hicks — $4.95
- ☐ 43114-8 **How to Reap Riches from Raw Land: Guide to Profitable Real Estate Speculation,** Glen Nicely — $3.45
- ☐ 43621-2 **How to Use Leverage to Make Money in Local Real Estate,** George Bockl — $3.95
- ☐ 44762-3 **The Human Side of Sales Management,** Burton Bigelow — $9.95
- ☐ 54889-1 **The Management of Time,** James T. McCay — $4.95
- ☐ 80420-3 **Sell Like an Ace — Live Like a King,** John H. Wolfe — $4.95
- ☐ 85875-3 **Study Guide for Real Estate License Examinations,** Ralph P. Ripley — $3.95
- ☐ 87789-4 **Surefire Sales Closing Techniques,** Les Dane — $4.95
- ☐ 91896-1 **36 Biggest Mistakes Salesmen Make and How to Correct Them,** George N. Kahn — $4.95

Prices subject to change without notice.

BUY THEM AT YOUR LOCAL BOOKSTORE OR USE THIS HANDY COUPON

REWARD BOOKS — Dept. 4
Book Distribution Center
Route 59 at Brook Hill Drive
West Nyack, New York 10994

Please send me the books I have checked above. I am enclosing $_____
(please add 50¢ per copy to cover postage and handling). Send check or money order — no cash or C.O.D.'s. Please allow 4 weeks for delivery.

PLEASE   Mr.   Mrs.
                Ms.   Miss
PRINT   Name ....
                (circle one)
OR   Address ....
TYPE   City .... State .... Zip ....

Dept. 4   BP 6811(7)